AuthorHouse™
1663 Liberty Drive
Bloomington, IN 47403
www.authorhouse.com
Phone: 1 (800) 839-8640

Published by AuthorHouse 08/23/2016

ISBN: 978-1-5049-7813-2 (sc)
ISBN: 978-1-5049-7814-9 (e)

SALES
PSYCHOLOGY
MILLION DOLLAR SALES SECRETS

NORMAN MEIER

authorHOUSE®

CHAPTER 1

SALES
PSYCHOLOGY
AND COMMUNICATION

Sales is the foundation for every business success

You need to understand human psychology so that you can position your products in the best possible way. You need to become a specialist in human behavior and develop your communicative abilities. Some people believe that you need to be born as a sales person. That is true: you need to be born first in order to become a sales person. This is good news because sales ability is a skill that can be learned. It is not something that you either have or don't have. It is a series of techniques that can be learned and developed. Everybody wants to be successful. It is not intelligence or knowledge that determines success. It is the ability of how someone can sell his ideas, products or himself.

There are a lot of sales people that earn more than a million dollars per year. This is not something that happens from one day to the next. It is a process and a development that someone had to go through. By improving each sales skill on a daily basis, you will get better and improve your results.

Why are some people more successful than others? It has to do with the law of cause and effect. Everything happens for a reason. Success and failure are both results of a specific cause that proceeded. If you want to have what other successful people have, then you must do the same things that they have done. And what others have done or achieved before you, you can do as well. You don't need to reinvent the wheel. You need to learn and copy those things that have made other sales people successful and you will be successful as well.

My story – why am I qualified to talk about this subject?

Why am I qualified to talk about sales? Here is a quick look at my story: at the age of 20 I got into straight commission sales in a financial planning sales organization. At the age of 21 I was earning $10,000 a month. By the time I was 23, I became the number one sales team leader in our company in Europe. There were 1000 other team leaders that I had to compete against. By that time I had hired and trained over 75 sales people. In the six years I was with this financial planning company I have had over 3000 face-to-face meetings with clients.

Eventually, I got so good at my job that I had a perfect closing rate for over nine months. Usually, my closing rate was somewhere between 80 and 90%. During that time my team and I had raised over $400 million in financial and insurance products.

I taught other sales people how to become better in sales. I taught them topics like sales techniques, communication, financial consulting and financial basics. Later, I was working for the largest independent hedge fund company in the world and with my sales team we raised over $245 million in four months. We raised the money from financial professionals, banks and institutional clients.

Later, I built my own companies and raised millions for them though Private Equity. I had several sales organizations and over 60 people working for me. This is not to brag but to show you that I have a lot of sales experience that you can benefit from.

Basics about communication

"Think like a wise man but communicate in the language of the people."
(William Butler Yeats)

There are always four factors that need to be followed in order to make a sale. The first factor is likeability. No one will ever buy from you if they don't like you. In order for someone to like you, you need to make sure that you are smiling, are open and positive and that you have a welcoming and warm attitude or aura.

Usually, you can develop likeability during small talk. Don't get straight to the point. Make sure that you develop rapport and that the other person likes you first. Show honest interest in the other person and give praise and recognition where it is possible and appropriate. You cannot proceed before you have laid a foundation of mutual likeability. If you skip this step, you will not sell anything.

The second factor is trust. A person will not buy from you if he or she doesn't trust you. They might like you but if they don't trust you, you will not sell anything.

You can develop trust by making sure that the way you look is appropriate, how you choose your words, how competent you appear, by the way you are dressed, by being referred by others, your educational level, your level of self-confidence and eye contact.

The problem is not necessarily what you do or say, it is the other person's sub-conscious that will determine whether or not they trust you. If the other person gets a bad feeling he or she will not trust you. When two people communicate with each other only 5% happens on a verbal level and the other 95% are non-verbal.

Imagine that each one of us carries a big old Neanderthal on our backs. The Neanderthal represents our sub-conscious. The Neanderthal is much bigger and stronger than we are and he decides in the end what happens. If you can't win the trust of the Neanderthal then you have lost. So the goal is to speak and act in such a manner that you can win the trust of the other person's Neanderthal.

The third factor is finding a need. It is possible that the other person likes you and that he or she trusts you but if they don't really have a need to do business with you, they will not buy from you, either. It's possible that your product might be ok but if the other person doesn't see a good reason for him or her to buy your product, then you won't sell it. In order for someone to see the need for a product, you need to show your client his or her deficit first. You need to make him or her aware of a deficit. That means that you need to explain or create awareness about the negative implications of not having or using your product.

You need to show your client that his current situation is not as ideal as he may think. Only if you create a deficit and make him aware that he has a problem, will you be able to sell something.

A good example is life insurance. Once the client is aware of the possible consequences that his death might have for his family, he will develop the need or desire to buy life insurance. Before that he would simply not worry about it.

And the last factor is price. Only after you have made sure that someone likes you, trusts you and has a need, then you are allowed to talk about the price. Everything else will kill the sale.

So let's summarize: LTNP

> **L**ikeability before **T**rust before **N**eed before **P**rice

The goal of a successful communication

This rule is a general rule that not only applies to your customers but is also valid in your relationship with your spouse:

> **said** ≠ heard ≠ **understood**   **understood** ≠ agreed
> **agreed** ≠ ready to do   **ready to do** ≠ stick with it

There can be a lot of misunderstandings when it comes to communication. If, for example, the wife tells her husband to take out the garbage, it does not guarantee that he will actually do it. Just because she has said it to him does not necessarily mean that he has heard or understood it. Even if he has understood it, it does not mean that he agrees. And even if he agrees, it does not mean that he is ready to do it now or to keep doing it.

In order to solve this dilemma you need to ask control questions. In sales or general communication you can simply never assume. You always need to get clarity. Only if you have clarity, you know where you stand. Therefore, you need to clarify each step along the way by asking your client control questions.

Communication is everything!

It is not important how much you know but how you apply it. People who are good communicators will earn more money and will generally be more accepted than others. Everything counts: your facial expressions, how you emphasize something, how you pronounce something, how fast you talk, how loud you talk and what words you use. How you use your language can make a huge difference.

Let's say you ask a client the following questions:
1. I have something very interesting for you where you can make a lot of money. Are you available tonight? Let's meet on 1200 Main Street.

You will have less success if you say the following:
2. Are you available tonight? Let's meet on 1200 Main Street – just across from the cemetery.

Or for example if a man says to a woman:
1. Every time I look into your eyes, time stands still.
2. When I see your face, every clock stops working.

Sometimes by simply changing around words, it can mean something completely different and the result will be different. Two religious people who are heavy smokers can ask for permission the two following ways:
1. Am I permitted to smoke while I pray?
2. Am I permitted to pray while I smoke?

Even though both ask basically the same thing, the answer and the result will be different.

Another factor might be how you are dressed. If you are in a jump suit that is full of oil and you try to convince someone of the advantages of a financial product, the outfit does not match the content of your conversation. No matter how good or important your content might be.

The same is true for the location of your conversation. Sometimes you should not discuss things in the restroom.

Learn and practice question techniques

"Don't ask a woman if you can kiss her. Either do it or don't do it.
But for God's sake don't ever ask a woman!"
(Umberto Saxer, sales trainer)

In every other case make sure you ask questions. (Ha, ha...)

People who ask questions control the conversation. Make sure that you only talk 30% of the time and that your client talks 70% of the time. When you ask questions you will find out everything you need to know in order to make a sale.

Great sales people have all questions carefully prepared and thought through. They ask high quality questions that are emotional and that keep the client's attention. Never be afraid to ask personal questions. But always ask politely and positively.

The great thing about our society is that we are conditioned to answer questions when someone asks us a question. Therefore, whoever asks questions, is leading the conversation.

Questions are a great way to extract information from a client. One technique is called the parrot technique. Like a parrot, you repeat the last word of a question that someone has asked you.

For example: If someone asks you if you are also dealing with derivatives but you have no idea what derivatives are, then you simply repeat the last word. You ask back: "Derivatives? What do you mean?" or "How do you mean?"

The client will then give you a more detailed form of his question. In that case you will gain time to consider your answer and be more accurate with it.

Types of questions

You need to use sales techniques and rhetorical questions in such a way that the client doesn't realize that you are using a technique.

• *Closed questions*

Closed questions always have a *"yes"* or *"no"* answer. It is either something positive or negative. For example: *"Is your last name Smith?"* or *"Are you going to the movies tonight?"*. You should try to avoid closed questions in a sales presentation. You might get the wrong answer and kill the sale.

• *Open questions*

Open questions are typically questions that start with *"how"*, *"what"*, *"who"*, *"where"* or *"why"*. These types of questions will give you lots of information about the client or his circumstances. Examples are: *"How did you get here today?"* (The bus) or *"What did you do after you got up this morning?"* (Brushed teeth and had a shower). Ask lots of open questions to find out more about the client.

• *Questions with options*

These types of questions always offer a choice between two options. Often you need to help a client to make a decision. Instead of asking him a closed question by saying something like *"would you like to do this deal?"* you rather give him two options. Ask: *"Would you prefer investing $20,000 or $30,000 into this product?"* You never give him the option to say *"no"*. His thoughts now focus on those two amounts and not whether he would like to do the deal or not.

• *Hypothetical questions*

These types of questions open up the client for new ideas and possibilities. Some of those questions are: *"Assuming you had a million dollars, what would you do with it?"* or *"Imagine there was no more Coca Cola, what would that mean for the world?"* or *"Would it not be better if we all had better sleep?"*

You can use these kinds of questions with closed up clients that initially don't show any interest in your products. You could ask: *"Assuming, I was able to show you a way how to double your money in twelve months, would you give me five minutes of your time?"*

• *Rhetorical questions*

Rhetorical questions are questions where its answer is already clear from the beginning. Examples are: *"Your name is Smith, isn't it?"* or *"You want to pay less taxes, don't you?"* or *"You wouldn't like it if someone hit you on the head, right?"*

These questions can be quite direct. You need to get a good feeling for when you can use them and when to let them be.

• *Suggestive questions*

In this case you try to imply something. These kinds of questions target things like honor, community, status or image. If you found out that there was something that is important to your client, then you can use that kind of question.

Examples: *"I am sure that an intelligent person like yourself doesn't like to see a situation like that, right?"* or *"You definitely want to do something against those ever raising taxes, don't you?"*

• *Control questions*

Control questions help you to make sure that your client has really understood all the things that you have mentioned during a presentation. If you just keep a monolog and never ask any control questions, you might risk losing the client somewhere along the way. That is why you need to frequently ask a control question to make sure every important topic or point has been understood and agreed upon.

Examples: *"Was this point clear so far?"* or *"Did you understand the importance of this point?"* or *"Has everything made sense so far?"*

• *Counter questions*

These types of questions will buy you time and give you more information before you have to give an answer back. Examples are: *"How do you mean?"* or *"What exactly do you mean by...?"*

The parrot technique is also a counter question technique.

Praise and recognition

> ***There are only two things that people want more than sex and money:***
> ***Praise and recognition!***
> (Mary Kay Ash)

Most people don't get enough praise and recognition in life. Make sure you give out lots and lots of praise when dealing with your clients. You will win a lot of people this way. A typical response should always start with praise. If someone asks you a question, you should always start with some of these expressions:

"That is an interesting question."
"Thank you very much for mentioning this."
"It's great that you mention that. Most people would never do that."

After that you should use an expression of understanding. This can be something like this:

"I can really understand this."
"I feel the same."
"I appreciate your honesty with me."
"I am not surprised that someone like you has so little time."
"I am sorry to hear that."
"I really feel for you."

And finally you ask a question back.

The formula is:
1. Praise and recognition
2. Expression of understanding
3. New question

Here's an example:

Client:
"This product seems too expensive!"

Answer:
"Thank you very much for mentioning that. I think it's great that you are so straightforward with me. Most people wouldn't do that. **(Praise and recognition)** *I am not surprised that you feel that this product seems expensive at first.* **(Expression of understanding)** *Assuming I was able to show you a product that offers a lot of advantages that others don't have, even though it was a bit more expensive, would you generally be open to have a look at it?"* **(New question that opens him)**

Understanding the psychology behind objections

> *The most curious animal in the world is not the cat. It is the human.*

Objections are normal. Nobody wants to buy a product at first. If you don't get objections, then there is no interest. Objections are nothing else but questions. If you get objections, then you should welcome them with open arms. They are buying signals.

• Objection example: "I have no interest"
Real meaning: You have failed to make the client curious. Curiosity is key when first dealing with new investors. You will have to make a statement that will tackle his curiosity.

The second reason might be that he is scared. In this case you will have to take out any kind of risk. The first approach with any new client has to be a non-threatening first contact. People are afraid that you will sell them something and that they are forced into something that they don't want.

You could say something like: *"I totally understand that you have no interest at this point in time. That is normal. I would suggest that it would be best if I will send you some general information that you can look at and then you can decide if you think this could be interesting for you. Does that sound fair?"*

The question at the end *"Does that sound fair?"* is a trick question. The question in itself will force the client to say *"yes"*. The proposal is of course fair. There is no other answer possible.

The main goal in the beginning is to simply get a first non-threatening contact established. Once you have sent him some information you have a reason to call him back. Sending him information is non-threatening and there is no obligation for him to do anything.

You can also say this: *"Mr. Smith, almost all of my clients have reacted exactly the same way like you just did. They also had no interest at first. But once they looked at the material and talked to me for a short period of time, they all realized how much money they could make. So let me make a suggestion: Why don't I send you some general information about a deal for you to study. And if you want to talk further, then we can talk. If not, no harm done. Does that sound fair?"*

Another option is: *"I can understand your reaction because you simply don't know yet what this is all about. Therefore I would suggest the following: I will send you some general information for you to look at and you can still decide later whether this is of interest to you or not. Does that sound fair?"*

• **Stay positive**

Objections are a normal part of the selling process. Don't get discouraged and welcome objections positively and with open arms. Say things like: *"Oh, Mr. Client, I knew you were going to say that! Ha, ha!"*. Don't ever get angry, disappointed or lose your happy mood.

> **Most people don't want to buy anything at first!**

Try two or three rebuttals with clients but if you feel that you are not getting anywhere, let them go and focus on the next client. You need to protect your integrity and your own motivation.

If there's one person who is overly negative he might destroy your motivation and spirit and you won't be able to talk to other clients with the same enthusiasm. You don't need negative people in your life. Sometimes it is better not to do a deal with someone if you get the feeling that this person will be difficult or trouble in the future.

• How do you deal with objections?

> *An objection is nothing but a question. It shows that the person is interested. The rule is: no objections = no interest*

Try to identify the real reason behind objections. If someone says that they have no money, it might not necessarily be true. They might be afraid to lose money or they feel that the little money that they have is not enough for an investment. Always try to prepare and answer potential objections in advance. It is ok to mention negative features of a product if you say them first. By doing this you will take away the persons argument later and he can't bring it up again.

Make a list of all the potential objections that clients bring up and prepare written answers. Learn those answers by heart so that you are better prepared when they come. The objections are always more or less the same and they are:

- I have no interest
- I have no money
- I have no time
- I already have a financial advisor
- I have lost money before
- This is too risky for me

- I already have a tax consultant
- I don't buy stocks over the phone
- I need to ask my wife
- I don't like this industry, product or the terms
- I need to think about it / sleep on it

You can also use all the rhetorical techniques in the world and "win" every argument with the client but if you lose the person, you won't be able to make a sale. Great sales people use techniques as well but only in such a manner that you cannot easily identify them as sales techniques. Great sales people use a lot of statements that trigger emotions. They focus mainly on the relationship with the client. A lot of great sales people try to find a deficit in the client's situation and then build this up and develop almost a problem situation for the client. Once the client is afraid, they will present the product as the solution to fix that problem and the client is happy.

> ### *When you get an objection, read between the lines. What does it really mean?*

If he says he has no money it does not necessarily mean that he has zero dollars. It could mean that he is afraid of losing money, he doesn't trust you or that he doesn't think that his savings of $200,000 would qualify him to be an investor. You need to find out the real reason behind an objection. Prepare all possible objections in advance. Write them down and create answers. The more possible arguments you have the more calm will you be.

Put yourself into your client's shoes. Empathize with him and try to feel where he is at emotionally. Show understanding for his situation and think about how you could move him into the right direction. Studies have shown that sales people who doubt their own products have gotten more objections using the same script as sales people who believe in their products. The only difference is their mental attitude.

Dealing with a conflict

If you try to win an argument with a client you can only lose. Don't try to convince your client by confronting him directly with your sales arguments. In a situation like that you need to first open up your client to your ideas by using the techniques that we just covered (praise and recognition, etc.)

If a client says: *"I don't need your product!"* you could reply like this: *"I am glad that you tell me this so directly. If I was in your shoes I would probably react exactly the same way."* (Praise and recognition, expression of understanding)

By giving this answer you move your client from a negative to a more neutral point of view.

You continue: *"Let me make the following suggestion: Assuming I knew something that would give you a tremendous financial advantage that you didn't know yet, wouldn't it make sense to spend at least five minutes on this topic? After you've had a chance to look at it, you can still decide whether or not this is right for you, agreed?"*

Psychologically it is important that you never say: *"You are wrong."* You might win the argument but lose the person. Therefore, you need to first take the client's point of view and say that you agree with him. Once you have done that you must encourage the client to see your point of view and let him realize how much better it is. Some people can be quite stubborn and they don't want to change their opinions. So you first must get on their side before they are ready to get on yours.

Practice makes perfect. Even though some of those types of questions seem complicated at first, it is important to practice them so that they become natural. Eventually, people will not realize that you are using a technique. So make sure you practice these techniques with your friends or your sales coach. It will make a big difference in your sales results!

Prospecting

> *The main reason why some people don't like*
> *to do prospecting is not necessarily the fear of rejection.*
> *The main reason is that they are simply not good at prospecting.*
> *Therefore decide to become the best at prospecting.*

General points

If you are doing no prospecting and suddenly switching to a lot of prospecting can be overwhelming. An easy to understand analogy is to imagine that you have never run in the past and you are going to take up running to get yourself into shape. Depending on your current physical condition, you start out with only a quarter mile. Eventually, you will be running longer distances.

Prospecting has a very predictable result. If you put more effort into the process, you will achieve a greater result. However, your success will never be immediate. Depending on the life cycle of the selling process, it may take a few weeks until you can see some results.

If you make 5 calls a day that equals 25 calls a week. If you take 50 weeks x 25 calls a week you end up with 1250 calls a year. Do you think you would sell more if you did additional 1250 calls a year?

Prospecting must be part of your daily activities, no matter what. If you are not successful at prospecting, it's unlikely you will be a successful salesperson. Remember that your database is your most valuable asset. It is important to have a system that will allow you keep track of all your prospects. Sales is always a numbers game. When you make 100 calls you will always have a result. For example:

100	Dials*	12	Proposals
50	Completed calls*	5	Sales
15	Appointments	$	20,000

Dials: the number of times you pick up the phone and press the number on your phone and it starts ringing. This also includes getting voice mail or the person's assistant.
Completed calls: This is when you actually reach the person intended and talk to him.

Most sales people are afraid of rejection. Most people try to avoid doing prospecting by procrastinating or doing endless research before they call up anybody. The trick is to alter your perceptions of prospecting and rejection. If your prospects would know exactly what you know about the product, they would buy it. Your job is to explain to them what you know.

A "no" is never final. Sometimes the time is simply not yet right for the client to do business with you. But that doesn't mean that they won't do business with you in the future.

> **A "no" is never final. You cannot lose a game when you control when it ends. You cannot lose what you never had.**

Preparation
• Create a positive atmosphere
• Put away everything from your desk except your calling list
• Have your appointment schedule ready

Set goals
• How many people do I want to talk to?
• What is the objective of each call? Sending out information or getting a meeting?
• How many meetings do I want to get?

Handling
• Watch your body posture. Sit straight or stand up.
• Keep the phone in front of your mouth. Make sure it is not on your neck.
• Remember that the most important thing is the client likes you at first. Therefore smile!
• Adjust your voice to the other person.
• Don't forget to pause on the right moments.

Mental attitude
It is normal that people will say "no" at first. Never take it personally! Remember that there is always a certain percentage of people who will buy your product in the end. The goal is simply to improve the number of people that will buy from you.

If, for example, it is your goal to get five appointments out of the 25 people that you call, then every "no" will bring you a step closer to your "yeses". Keep a positive attitude until you have completed your 25 calls.

Remember also the benefits of the product that you are selling. You are helping your clients to do better. If you are in a bad mood, you should take a break. Your client can feel if you are not happy or motivated on the other side of the line. Only make phone calls with a happy, energetic and positive attitude.

Create curiosity

Think about how you can incorporate curiosity into your sales process. You could ask the following questions:

- *"What would it mean to you if you had all of a sudden more money?'*
- *"Assuming I was able to show you a way to save more taxes, would that be of interest to you?"*
- *"Let's open up an account, put zero dollars into it and after five years you will have $13,000. Would you like to know how that works? Well then let's schedule an appointment."*

It is ok to be provocative in certain situations.

What is the main objective of your call?

> *The main objective of a call is to get a meeting – nothing else. Don't try to convince your client or sell anything in the first call.*

Typical call structure

1. Introduction
2. Reason for calling
3. Introduction of your services
4. Create curiosity
5. Make a proposal

Reason for calling

- *"My name is Norman Meier. Does that ring any bells yet? No? Well then let me introduce myself."*
- *"My name is Norman Meier. You probably have already heard my name. No? Well then let me introduce myself."*
- *"We have a mutual friend: Mr. Smith. He told me to give you a call and give you his regards. – Thank you!"*
- *"Just the other day I was able to show him a great investment opportunity. He told me that I absolutely had to call you as well and let you know about it. He was very excited about the opportunity."*

Important points

- Create a positive mood! Nothing is more important than to have a positive conversation.
- Let the prospect know that there is no obligation.
- Try to get a lot of "yeses".
- It is normal for people to be skeptical at first. Don't let that discourage you.
- Write down the most common objections and create good answers.

Handling objections on the phone

- ### *"I am not interested!"*

Real translation: The client doesn't yet know what you know. You either haven't created enough curiosity or he is still afraid. Give him time and don't push him. Suggest that he should first look at the marketing material and then he can still decide whether or not he wants to invest.

Suggested answers:

"I can understand that at this point you are not interested. That is totally normal. This is because you don't know yet exactly what I have to offer. Let me make a suggestion: why don't we have a short meeting and I can explain to you a little bit in detail and with documents what I mean exactly and then you can still decide whether or not this is of interest to you. Is that a fair suggestion?"

"I can understand how you must feel. I am calling you out of the blue and you think that I am just trying to sell you something. But that is not the case. I am a financial professional and I have helped a lot of people to improve their financial situation. Most people react with skepticism at first but after they get to know me, they don't regret having dealt with me. So let me make a suggestion: In order for you to get a feeling of whether or not I am worth spending some time with, I will send you some information about a product that will go public next year. It is extremely hot right now and the offer is very attractive. Why don't you have a look at the info that I am going to send you and I will give you a call in a few days to answer any questions you might have? Is that a fair proposal?"

- **"I have no money!"**

Two options: Either the client really has no money or he is afraid. The level of trust at this point is still very weak. It is possible that the prospect doesn't see a need at this point in time. Don't try to argue with the prospect. Ask him some questions to find out more about his situation.

"Thank you for being so honest with me. Let me make the following suggestion..."

- **"I have no time!"**

Real translation: He doesn't want to be bothered and lose time because he doesn't see the benefit at this point in time.

Answer:
- I am not surprised that someone like you is very busy and has very little time. Because of that you will only take time out of your busy schedule if it is really something worthwhile, correct?
- Correct!
- In that case I assume that you would only be interested in a very short conversation, am I right?
- Right!
- Well then I suggest that we only meet for 15 minutes and I show you exactly what I have to offer. After that you can still decide whether or not you want to invest more time into that, agreed?
- Agreed!

- **"What it is and how does it work exactly?"**

Note: If you give him any kind of information at this point in time, you will kill the sale. The question shows that he is curious but your objective is to get the meeting.

Answer: *"Your question shows me that you seem very interested in getting further information. It would make more sense if we meet for a short 15 minutes and I can explain to you in detail what this is all about. When is it most convenient for you next week?"*

- **"I lost money before!"**

Real translation: This means that he is afraid to make another mistake. In that case you need to be careful and try to build up trust. You could mention things like the size of your company, reputation and so on. You won't be able to convince him in the first meeting to buy your product. Ideally, you need to set up a personal meeting.

Answer: *"I am sorry to hear that. I am sure your advisor back then did not do it on purpose and he must not have done his due diligence properly. In our case the situation is a lot different. We have raised over $200 million from private investors in the last ten years and not in a single case did we get a complaint or lawsuit of any kind. You can imagine that we must deal with a lot of clients and that we make sure that the products that we offer are extremely well analyzed and selected. In order for you to get a better idea of what it is that we do and what we offer I would suggest that we have a short meeting and I can explain to you how it works exactly. Does that sound fair?"*

- **"My friend already works as a broker!"**

Answer: *"I am not surprised that you already know a broker. Most of my clients have really good brokers already. Please understand that I don't want you to change brokers. You can still continue to work with him and keep your assets there. The difference is that I have something to offer that he cannot offer. Our company specializes in pre-IPO financings and the deals that we take public are exclusively offered through our company. Can I make the following suggestion: Why don't I send you some basic information about a current deal that we are taking public and you can have a look at it. Does that sound fair?"*

Emotional intelligence and relationship management

All top sales people are without exception experts in building relationships.

Customers have changed and become more educated today. They are better informed and the request higher levels of service. Competition has increased and become stronger. And there are a lot more products out in the market and on the Internet than ever before.

In order to be successful in today's market you need to realize that the most important factor is your relationship with your clients.

If you focus on the relationship, your product will sell. But if you put your focus on the product rather than the relationship, you won't get very far.

There is a thing called the friendship factor. A person will not buy from you if they are not convinced that you are a good friend and that you will act in his best interest. Before you can even talk about the product, you must ensure that you have built trust and a good relationship.

There are different types of intelligence. The most important kind for a sales person and a good communicator is emotional intelligence. A person who has high levels of emotional intelligence can feel what the clients' worries and emotions are. He is aware that the focus of every conversation must lie on building the relationship and that everything that he says will have an influence on the clients' reaction.

Someone with high levels of emotional intelligence will realize when the mood changes and then can react to the situation accordingly. In the end, only sales people who are sensitive enough to feel other people will be successful. When a conversation is difficult, one wrong word or statement can kill a sale.

But it is also when sales people are clueless about their own blabbering when the client seems bored when emotional intelligence is needed. In that case you need to change your approach and start speaking more dynamically. Ask yourself what kind of influence your statements will have on the client. Will you offend him? Will it improve the mood? How will he feel about it?

Emotional intelligence can be trained and developed. The more sensitive you get and the more you can find out how it made someone else feel when you asked a question, the more will you be able to change your approach and chose your language wisely.

Hypnotic suggestions

When most people think about hypnosis they imagine a show on a stage or a person putting someone into a deep sleep to recall memories or similar things. But hypnosis is much more than that.

> *Hypnosis is a way to touch or communicate with our sub-conscious mind.*

It is a series of techniques that most successful sales people use but they don't even know that they are using them. Just as a hypnotist is using calm and repetitive words to communicate, so do top sales people use language or techniques to create certain emotions in the customers.

Depending on how things are being pronounced, it can have an effect on the client. If the word is being spoken in a slow, calming and repetitive manner, it will increase the momentum of the effect.

One very powerful hypnotic technique is called the "posthypnotic suggestion". The hypnotist tells a person a series of actions and the final action will be almost like an order.

It goes something like this: *"I will count down from ten to one and once I have reached one, you will be completely relaxed and in a deep sleep. Once you are in this relaxed state, I will give you..."*

Now, in a sales situation, the posthypnotic suggestion could be something like this: *"Mr. Client, tonight, when you go home* (= truth), *you will put your head on your pillow* (= truth) *and then you will think about our conversation once again* (= suggestion). *You will remember all the positive features of our product and then you will go to sleep in a completely relaxed state. The next morning when you wake up* (= truth) *you will realize that it is the right decision and then you will give me a call to confirm the order* (= suggestion)."

> ### All top sales people use those kinds of techniques, whether they're aware of them or not.

A lot also depends on your intonation and emphasis on certain words. If you repeat a word and emphasize it slowly you will "touch" the other person more deeply. Example: *"Once you buy this product, you will have more and more and more joy."*

There is an excellent book about this technique by Donald Moine and Kenneth Lloyd called *"Unlimited Selling Power"*. One of the best sales books in my opinion.

Apply NLP (Neuro Linguistic Programing)

NLP stands for Neuro Linguistic Programming. It is a behavioral method that was developed by Dr. Richard Bandler and Dr. Binder. Anthony Robbins used to be their assistant. It is about a series of techniques that you can learn to be more influential with other people. You will be able to build trust much faster and therefore be able to influence your customer.

One of the basic modules is building rapport. You can build rapport by behaving in a similar manner like your client.

You can use the same kind of tone when you speak, the same speed, use the same expressions, breathe in the same rhythm or be physically in the same position like your client. All these factors help your client to feel more comfortable with you because we trust and like the things that are similar to us. Try to "mirror" the behavior and physical movements of your clients and you will be amazed how much faster they will start to trust you. Some people sell themselves more effectively than others. They seem to know naturally how to influence and persuade. As much as they might want to believe this ability is part of their personal charm, it is really the result of using a set of skills effectively.

In the 1970's, a project was begun to identify the skills that enable one person to quickly and consistently persuade another. This collection of skills was eventually called NLP. The name implies the power of the skills: the way the mind or neurology works has an effect on what we say, feel, and think.

NLP skills are valuable for influencing anyone anywhere. Discover the power of NLP and give yourself the power of the real unfair advantage: YOU. Learn the techniques to establish trust and rapport. It can improve your sales results and how you deal with other people in general.

How buyers buy

At first, no one wants to buy your products and services. That is normal. We are all swamped with too many sales offers these days.

People will buy products based on how it will make them feel. People will buy products if it makes their lives easier, more comfortable, makes the process go faster, makes it more beautiful or save more money. There are five questions that need to be answered in every sales presentation so that the customer will buy from you:

1. Why should I listen to you?   4. Who says so (except you)?
2. What it is? What can it do?   5. What is in it for me?
3. Who else has bought it?

Most people don't want to have big changes. They want to make sure that other people have also bought the product and that there are testimonials of happy clients, articles from newspapers and pictures.

People are driven by two main motivations:

1. To gain pleasure   2. To avoid pain.

Everything we do is based on these two principles.
If we associate more positive emotions with a certain product,
we are more likely to buy it. But if the product helps us to avoid pain,
we are equally if not even more motivated to buy the product.

A good sales person must create a lot of both kinds of emotions in his sales presentation by using statements and questions that trigger certain emotions.

People are also more likely to buy from someone who is a specialist in his field or an authority. They tend to trust a person much more if they position themselves as an expert.

People will also buy if you use three techniques:

1. Make it rare   2. Contrast principle   3. Time pressure

If a product is rare, it makes it much more valuable and desirable. People want things that are special and rare because it sets them apart from the crowd and makes them feel special.

The contrast principle gives you the feeling like you are getting a deal. If the price of a product is $100 at first and you perceive it to be a lot of money but then you can get it for $50, you feel like it is cheap now and then you will buy it.

Often, you will see this technique being used in infomercials. The price gets cut more and more the longer the infomercial is going on and in the end you will even get the twice the amount of the product for the lower price.

If you have to act until a certain deadline or else you will lose the opportunity to get the product, you are more likely to buy it. In the infomercial you will hear a statement like this: *"But you must act now within the next 10 minutes or else the offer will be gone."*

So they are using all three techniques and make people buy the product.

How to win friends and influence people

> *Every successful person is automatically a great sales person and communicator. Once you've understood this principle, you'll always be successful – no matter what you do.*

The greatest book on communication "How to win friends and influence people" was written by Dale Carnegie in the year 1936 and everything in it is still true for dealing with people today. No matter if you want to be successful in business or in your private life, this book has changed my life and the lives of many others in a positive way. This book is the foundation for learning and understanding other people and how to best interact with them. I have made a short summary for you with the most important rules.

- *How to deal with other people*

1. Don't criticize, judge or condem
No one likes to be around people who are constantly negative or criticizing everything and everybody. People who criticize others will eventually be alone in life. No one likes criticism. Even if you win with your arguments, you will lose the person.

2. Give honest praise and recognition
People don't get enough praise and recognition. If there is something positive that you can say to someone, do it. The reward you will get in return will be much greater.

3. Motivate and encourage other people

Motivate and encourage other people to fulfill their dreams and wishes. Once you have helped them, they will turn around and try to help you.

- ### *How to become popular*

1. Show an honest interest in the other person

Every person wants to be important. If you show an interest in the other person, you will get a lot more recognition. The idea is to ask a lot of questions and don't talk about yourself too much. Let the other person talk more while you listen.

2. Smile

The world is full of negative and unhappy people. If you smile, you will attract other people. Just like the quote: Laugh and the world will laugh with you. Weep and you weep alone.

3. The other person's name is the most important word for them

Always repeat his or her name and if you have forgotten it, don't be afraid to ask for it again. You will always be welcomed with open arms.

4. Be a good listener

Always ask questions. As a general rule, the other person should talk about 70% of the time and you should only talk about 30%. People will say that it is great to have a conversation with you even though you might not have given him much information about yourself.

5. Talk about the things that interest the other person

If you want to win the other person you must talk abou the things that interest him.

6. Help him to increase his level of self-confidence

People need praise and recognition to build their level of self-confidence. Help them and they will always stand by your side.

- **How to convince others**

1. The only way to win an argument or a fight is to avoid it

In an argument there are only losers. Every one wants to be right and forget that they destroy the relationship by wanting to be right. It is often much better to avoid an argument altogether.

2. Respect the opinion of the other person and never say: *"You are wrong!"*

If someone is convinced of his opinion but you know that he or she is wrong, then don't criticize him or her and make him feel bad. Often a person with a strong opinion is missing an important piece of information to change his opinion. Therefore, you should tell him that he is right from a particular point of view but encourage him to see your side as well. Make sure that he never loses his face.

3. If you are wrong, admit it immediately

Nothing is worse than fighting a fight that you cannot win because you're wrong and don't want to admit it. If you realize that you were wrong, admit it immediately so that the situation will be resolved quickly.

4. Always try it with friendliness

If you want to achieve something, use common sense and most of all be friendly. People who push and use anger will almost never get what they want.

5. Give others the opportunity to say *"yes"*

If you are in a conflict you must always make the first step and meet the other person half way. You will only get a positive reaction from the other person if you make a first move.

6. Let the other person talk most of the time

The more information you can gather by letting the other person talk, the more can you use it to achieve your goals. You will know how to better communicate and what strategy to use.

7. Let the other person believe that it was his idea

If you want to convince someone of your idea or plan, you must slowly develop and build up the conversation in such a way that the conclusion seems to be coming from him.

8. Try to honestly see his point of view

Sometimes it is difficult to understand and to accept an opinion from another person. Try to put yourself into his or her shoes and at least try to understand why he or she is thinking or acting that way. By doing that you will develop a lot more understanding which will have a positive result in your communication.

9. Encourage positive suggestions

Always praise good intentions or positive suggestions. The more positive the mood and atmosphere is around you, the more positive inputs will come your way.

10. Encourage him to set a higher standard and nobler motives

Deep down no one is a bad person. Even a criminal justifies his behavior. If you try to use common sense and encourage the other person to change his negative actions, he will be much more open to accept them.

- *How to change people without offending them*
1. Always start with praise and recognition
2. Begin with praise and honest appreciation.
3. Call attention to people's mistakes indirectly.
4. Talk about your own mistakes before criticizing the other person.
5. Ask questions instead of giving direct orders.
6. Let the other person save face.
7. Praise the slightest improvement and praise every improvement.
8. Give the other person a fine reputation to live up to.
9. Use encouragement. Make the fault seem easy to correct.

Behavioral patterns to make buying decisions

Have you ever lost your keys in your house? Do you remember what you did in that situation?

You first looked in the places where your keys would most likely be: Next to the door, in your jacket, in the kitchen, in the drawer and so on. But what did you do after you still didn't find your keys? You started to look AGAIN next to the door, AGAIN in your jacket, AGAIN in the kitchen, AGAIN in the drawer and so on.

You were searching in the exact same places like you did before several times. Isn't that crazy? You just checked in a place and you still didn't find it. The answer is simple. All people function according to certain patterns in their behavior. Almost everything that we do is a pattern. 95% of all our decisions are based on a program that has the same criteria in our heads.

When it comes to buying things, it is exactly the same. We all buy things according to a pattern and we make our buying decisions always the same way. Here is a combination of all possible patterns that people use:

- **Pattern 1: Who makes the decision?**
1. Make decision yourself
2. Influenced by others or what others say
3. Based on information

Let's say you wanted to book a trip with a travel agency. Some people can make that decision by themselves, others must first hear from others that the trip can be recommended and others will make the decision based on the fineprint in the brochure. Do you remember what you did in that situation?

- **Pattern 2: Similar — Yes, but... - Opposite**
80% of people will buy things that are similar to things that they already know. We are all creatures of habit and we feel most comfortable if things are similar or familiar. If you need to replace your sofa, you are most likely to buy a sofa that has a similar style. But there are people who do exactly the opposite of what is being presented to them. Those kinds of people are called "polarity responders". Those are very special kind of people who almost feel the need to do the opposite.

And finally, there is the type that constantly says: *"Yes, but..."* Those kinds of people will basically agree to your proposal but they always have to add one or two critical points or remarks. They will say things like: *"Your product is working fine and all but the service really needs improvement."* Those people always have to add their opinion and be critical. But they can't help it because it is their pattern.

In order for you to best deal with a client, you must find out what kind of person your client is. If he likes things that are the same, you should focus on features that are similar to what he is used to from the past.

If you get the polarity responder, you have to explain to him the features of the product and then take it away in the end. You should say things like: *"But this istn't for you."* Or *"This product is too expensive for you and therefore I don't recommend it to you."* Once you take it away or make it unavailable for him or tell him why it is not good for him, then he wants it even more. If you get the *"Yes, but..."* – type, then you should mention a few negative points of the product in advance and then he will respond: *"Yes, but it also has some positive points..."* and he will basically tell you all the reasons why it is good and he will sell it to himself.

- **Pattern 3: General or details?**

Most people simply want general information about a product. They want to know how it works and what kind of advantage they will get. But there are some people who absolutely NEED to know every little detail about the product including the fineprint. They want to see numbers, proof, statistics and other detailed information so that they can make a decision. Depending on which type you are dealing with, you need to be able to show the necessary details. But if you get the general type you risk boring the client with too many unnecessary details.

- **Pattern 4: Past or future?**

If you're selling a financial product, some people will focus on the past performance and they will assume that the product will have a similar performance going forward. Other people are focused on the future and new opportunities or chances. The future outlook is much more important to them than the history.

- **Pattern 5: Avoid problem or goal orientation?**

If you are selling any type of insurance you are trying to avoid a problem that might happen in the future. Other people focus on the goal and what they can accomplish if they buy the product.

- **Pattern 6: Structure or random?**

Some people need to follow a predefined plan or have a certain structure in place in order for them to make a buying decision. They MUST follow a certain order so that they can move forward. Others are more spontaneous and they don't care about structure.

- **Pattern 7: Cost, time or quality?**

The three factors of cost, time and quality can never be achieved at the same time. Sometimes things must go fast but the quality might suffer or it will cost more. Someone might have a great quality but it will take longer until it can be delivered. For some people cost is not important if he can get the product faster. That is why you must find out from your client where his priorities lie. Simply ask him.

- **Pattern 8: Visual, auditiv or kinesthetic?**

80% of people are visual. They want to see the product. They want to see a lot of picutres in your presentation. But there are also people who must hear that a product is good. And some must feel if the product is suitable. When someone is buying a car, the visual person looks at the prospectus and the pictures. The person who is auditiv wants to hear the engine and the kinestic person (feeling-oriented) wants to sit in the car, feel the leather and smell the new car smell.

Everyone has a different channel or method on how they perceive the car. You can find out what their preference is by hearing their statements like:

Visual: This looks good / I can see that... / If viewed from...
Auditiv: Sounds good / I have heard that... / Please tell me...
Kinestetic: Feels good / I have a good feeling... / I can feel...

- ### *Summary*

You must find out what kind of buying patterns are important to your potential client so that you can help him to make a decision. You can find out by asking him questions about past purchases. For example: When he bought his house or his car what were the factors that led to his decision? Here is a checklist again:

Pattern 1: Self, others, information?   Pattern 5: Avoid problem or goal orientation?

Pattern 2: Similar – Yes, but... - Opposite?   Pattern 6: Structure or random?

Pattern 3: General or details?   Pattern 7: Cost, time or quality?

Pattern 4: Past or future?   Pattern 8: Visual, auditiv or kinesthetic?

Dealing with objections in advance

Every product has positive and negative features. Most sales people make a presentation and only mention the positive features of a product hoping that the client will not notice or bring up the negative points.

This is not a very good strategy if you are trying to sell a product or if you want to build a relationship of trust. Sooner or later your client will find out about the negative features and then it is much harder to explain yourself.

Some negative features are also very difficult to try to make them appear positive.

The best strategy is to have control over how you communicate negative features of a product. You should mention them in the beginning of your presentation so that they don't get too much weight in the end. You need to take away the client's arguments and take away his objections in advance so that he can't bring them up later.

Let me make an example: *"Mr. Client, our product is the most expensive product in the market. But that is with good reason. Our product has features that the competition doesn't have. Would you be willing to hear what those are?"*

At that point, the client will not talk about the price anymore. It will not be an issue any longer and he will actually listen to the positive features. This strategy will give you more trust and the client won't have an opportunity to use this argument against you later on.

Simplicity and clarity

> ## *KISS = Keep it simple and stupid*

Most people understand thing best if they are simple and easy to understand. The more complicated you explain things; the less likely are people able to follow and understand you. Only about 10% of all people focus on details and read every single word of the prospectus. That is why you should keep your marketing material simple and easy to understand.

If your marketing material doesn't pass the cleaning lady test, then it is too complicated. If you have a cleaning lady who has no degree and is not particularly educated, then you should give her your marketing material to read. If she doesn't get it right away, then you should rewrite your materials.

It is an art to simplify complicated things and present them in such a way that everybody can understand them. The world is already complicated enough. The more simple and clear you can be, the better.

Credibility

Most people are scared to make a wrong decision. They are worried that they will pay too much for a product or service or buy a product that is not right for them. People are worried that their friends will ridicule them if they bought the wrong product. People worry that they won't get the product repaired or that there is no service after the purchase.

Everything that you say or do will either increase the trust and credibility or lower it. Take away people's fear. People are even willing to pay more to avoid risk.

The first impression is responsible for 95%. The way you are dressed, how you present yourself, the quality of your marketing materials and how successful your company is, are all factors that will help with your credibility.

People need to hear that you have been in business for 20 years, that you have over 1000 clients or that you belong to a certain organization. It is important for them to know how big your market share is and what the company's reputation is.

People like to deal with the best or with specialists.

If the masses approve of your company then it will be much easier for you to sell. That is why testimonials are also an important factor. Your sales and marketing material must be absolutely perfect so that you don't lose trust and credibility. You can also use proof or picutres of happy clients. You can let people know which products are most popular and which ones are less popular. The more proof and credibility you can provide, the better. Remember: Everything counts!

Emotions

Use words, stories and pictures that trigger emotions.

95% of all buying decisions are made on an emotional level. If that weren't true, we would all drive the Russian car Lada. Once they said that the Lada car was the most efficient in regards to price, gas, repairs, etc. However, how many of those cars do you see on the roads?

We are all driven by emotions and the more you are able to touch someone on an emotional level, the more successful you will be in selling your products. Most people are scared or worried and you need to make emotional statements or tell stories that go deeper.

It is of course also important to give facts and numbers so that you can come full circle. But the rational information is only so that he can feel good about his decision.

The kinds of words that you use will influence people's emotions, perceptions or attitudes. Words create emotions and make people feel a certain way. That is why it is important HOW you say things. Sometimes you need to use different words in your sales presentation to avoid negative associations. Instead of the word "pay" you can use the word "save". It is basically the same action but the association is different.

> *A negative description can also influence someone's emotional state and his motivation to take action.*

If you are trying to sell a life insurance product and you tell your client that his wife and kids will have no money in the event of his death and that they have to eat dry bread, live in a dark one bedroom apartment with only one table and a rat is crawling across the floor because it is so cheap, then you will have created or painted a picture that is very emotional and that will get him to take action.

Symbols, music or smells will also trigger emotions or associations. People connect certain symbols with certain values. They can be positive or negative. Americans, for example, are very patriotic and the eagle is a symbol for freedom and independence. If your product has an eagle on the label, then people will associate those values and emotions with your product.

If you want to convey a sense of trust, then you should chose the color dark blue. We tend to relate and connect things that are trustworthy with this color. If you used bright yellow or poison green, it won't be helpful to you.

Words that trigger emotions

What do people want most of all? Many psychologists have asked themselves the same question. Here is a list with the main motivations:

- More money
- Lower cost
- Convenience

- Beauty
- Ego
- Position and recognition

- Speed

People want a certain "feeling" that they can associate with buying a product. That is why you should focus on one of these things when you position your product. Certain words can trigger certain emotions in us and will be more effective than others. Here is a list of words that help to sell your products:

- You
- New
- Now
- Guarantee
- Money

- Secure
- Fast
- Only
- How to...

- Win
- Save
- Breakthrough
- Secret

It is important that you use words in your titles or slogans that will trigger emotions. Here is a list of examples:

- 11 secrets how to be more popular
- Why certain foods explode in your stomach
- How to build a dream body

The goal is to communicate the value for the customer just like in "What is in it for me?" rather than the features of the product.

How to motivate and influence people

A great sales person is also a great psychologist.

There are a number of techniques that will influence people more effectively and will touch them on an emotional level. These techniques can be extremely powerful. If you apply these principles and techniques, you will become one of the most successful sales people.

> *A great sales person understands what motivates other people, knows their needs, gives praise and recognition and increases their level of self-confidence.*

School is supposed to prepare our children for life. Unfortunately, most things that they learn are not useful for the daily working life. Things like communication, sales or psychology are missing in the curriculum.

The interesting thing is that most people function in a similar way. Most people have the same motivations, behaviors, emotions or thoughts. Once you have fully understood what drives and motivates most people, you will never look at the world the same way.

The knowledge of sales psychology and communication can be very powerful and it can influence other people. We constantly need to sell ourselves to our clients, our boss, our family members or friends. Basically, selling is to understand the psychological basics on how to interact with other people.

Sales techniques are tools that can help to convey certain messages or to trigger certain emotions. But you need to be careful when applying techniques. If someone realizes that you are using a technique, you will achieve the opposite of what you originally wanted.

Therefore your intentions are vital and people will feel if you have their best interest at heart.

My advice to you is to learn everything about sales psychology and the techniques to influence other people. Become an expert in communication and sales. Learn everything there is to know about these topics. If you do that well, there is no limit to what you can achieve in business and in life.

Basic elements of selling

In selling, there are basic elements that you need to master. Just like a tennis player needs to work on his basic elements like volley, serve, backhand or forehand, you need to master all the basic elements in selling. Here are the basic elements:

1. Sales techniques and rhetoric
2. Building relationships and rapport
3. Building trust
4. Prospecting

5. Presenting
6. Needs analysis
7. Dealing with objections
8. Closing

The basic elements are things that need to be trained and repeated on a regular basis. But just as important is the mental attitude of the sales person. 20% of the things that you do will bring you 80% of your results. The law of cause and effect states that if you do the things that other successful top sales people do, you will achieve the same results. So find out what they are doing. Ask for advice and follow it.

The topic of sales is a means to an end. Selling is a tool that can help you to achieve your personal goals. You can calculate how much money you want to make by applying the numbers game in the basic areas.

The better you become in each basic area the higher will be your sales results. Some sales people even motivate themselves by calculating the amount of meetings they need to make in order to buy their dream car. They know what their numbers are in each area and by putting in enough efforts in the beginning of the sales process they will be able to calculate the results.

The only thing holding you back in selling is fear. Fear of failure and fear of rejection are the two biggest enemies of sales people. Once you have overcome those two fears everything is possible.

Top sales people need to be professional in everything that they do. They focus on the client's needs and are never lazy when it comes to communicating with their clients. They see themselves as problem solvers and not as high-pressure sales people.

And the final characteristic of top sales people is their high level of responsibility. They know that they are the only ones responsible for their results and success. No one else is responsible or to blame. It is not the boss, the company, the clients or the market. The responsibility always lies with the sales person.

> **80% (100%) of success comes
> from mental attitude and only 20% are skills.**

Selling laws and principles

If someone plays a wrong tune on the piano we start to crinch. The law of disharmony states that if a person is in a situation that feels uncomfortable or wrong that we have the need to correct the situation. The main goal in selling is to create a situation where the client sees a deficit. Only if he has a deficit he will develop a need and therefore a motivation to change his situation.

If a product is rare and chances are that you will lose it if you don't act now, you are more motivated to act. If there is no time pressure or pressure that it will no longer be available, then there is little motivation to act now. The mere thought of losing a potential deal and later feeling sorry about it will drive many people to buy a product quickly.

Without rapport and the friendship factor there is no sale possible. If you smile, dress well and show interest in the other person you will be much more successful in achieving your goals. Make sure that the other person will like you.

If you walk into a carpet store in the Middle East, you will first be greeted friendly and then offered a coffee or tea. Once you received that "gift" you are more likely to want to reciprocate and buy a carpet for a $1000. If there is a situation where there is a disbalance we tend to want to put it back in order. So make sure to give your clients small presents, give out compliments or do some special favors.

The contrast principle is the most common and most used method in selling. Typical statements go something like this: "Normally this product costs $10,000 but today it is only $2500!" Depending on the product $2500 might still be a lot but if you put it in relation to $10,000 it appears to be a deal and cheap. Some products are broken down to a fraction of the total amount.

Things like "Just for a dollar a day" make it appear very affordable. And sometimes a bigger payment gets split up in 3 or 4 payments to make it seem lower. 4 payments of $24.95 sound a lot less than one big payment of $100.

The law of involvement is also very commonly used. If you give out free samples or if you only ask for 10 minutes of the client's time, you are halfway to your goal. Often it gets harder for people to get out of the sales process once they are in it. Therefore the goal of every phone call is not to convince the client of the product but only to get the appointment. Once you get your foot in the door, you have got it made in most cases.

Often companies use celebrities to help sell their products. Automatically we associate positive feelings and trust with this person. Those feelings get projected to the company and its products. If the celebrity is working with this company, there is almost no more restistance from the buyers because they automatically trust the company.

Excitement and fire are some of the most powerful weapons of sales people. If the sales person is on fire and excited about the company, it has an effect on the clients. The spark will go over to the client and he will get excited as well.

And finally our two main motivations that drive us: to gain pleasure or to avoid pain.

We tend to be more motivated to avoid a certain situation and the fear of it is often the stronger motivation than the chance of gaining pleasure. Top sales people are experts in triggering emotions that potentially can make people afraid.

Final words and secrets of success in selling

- Decide the become the best
- Decide to keep learning and improving your sales skills
- Make prospecting your number one skill in selling
- Surround yourself with other great sales people and avoid negative people
- Always think positive thoughts and expect the best possible outcome
- Learn from failure and keep getting better
- Become a role model for others

CHAPTER 2

PRINCIPLES OF
INFLUENCE
AND
MOTIVATIONAL
PSYCHOLOGY

The science of influencing others

Influencing others isn't luck or magic – it's science.

School is supposed to prepare our children for life. But instead they learn things that won't help them in real life. Most subjects in school have little to do with practical use in every day life. Studies have shown that 95% of a person's success depends on his ability to communicate with other people. But the topics of communication, sales or rhetoric are missing in schools.

Most people underestimate the job of a sales person. Most of them tend to have a negative image or association with sales people. But in reality every one of us is a sales person. You are constantly selling yourself or your ideas. You are selling yourself to your boss, to your spouse or your friends.

Selling is basically nothing else but effective communication.
If you want something, you need to communicate it
and follow basic psychological laws.

Interestingly, most people function based on the same principles. We all have the same motivations, behavioral patterns, emotions or thoughts. Once you have understood all these psychological factors you can use them to influence others. Once you have understood the basic principles and secrets, the world will never be the same.

Being able to influence other people is power. You will have the power to get what you want by influencing other people. And it doesn't matter if it is your clients, family or co-workers.

Being able to communicate effectively can make you a lot of money. Top sales people use a lot of these techniques to earn six or seven income figures. Marketing professionals know and understand what messages will trigger buying signals and therefore they can use that approach in their businesses.

In order to influence someone you need to touch him or her on an emotional level.

In this program you will learn the basic techniques to motivate and influence other people. The goal is to apply them with integrity so that you can achieve your personal and financial goals as an entrepreneur, businessman or sales person.

If you include these techniques in your sales presentations or marketing material you will be more successful than ever before.

Influencing others isn't luck or magic — it's science. There are proven ways to influence other people. And it doesn't matter whether you are a marketing expert, sales person or a politician. In order to influence and persuade someone there are a number of principles and techniques that need to be applied. The customers' ability to understand the factors that affect their behavior is surprisingly poor. Most people can't explain why they made a particular decision.

The following is a summary of techniques and principles to help sales people to persuade clients. But this knowledge is not about trying to push low-quality good or set unfair prices.

Like anything in life, if techniques are used in an unethical way to gain something in the short-term, it will always have negative consequences in the long run. The principles are very powerful but they only work when good intentions are applied. You can't really sell something to someone that he doesn't need or that isn't in some way good for him.

But those techniques will certainly help to boost your sales, close more deals and create more happy customers if you have a good product that makes sense.

Scarcity

People want what they can't have.

In fundamental economic theory, scarcity relates to supply and demand.

Basically, the less there is of something, the more valuable it is. The more rare and uncommon a thing, the more people want it. Familiar examples are frenzies over the latest holiday toy or urban campers waiting overnight to get the latest iPhone.

> *If your product or service is genuinely unique, be sure to emphasize its unique qualities to increase the perception of its scarcity.*

People always want what they can't have. They want it if it is rare or special. If you position your products as rare and exclusive, they will become more valuable. People will be more motivated to buy them.

People don't want to miss out on an opportunity

> *People hate to lose an opportunity.*

Therefore, it may be worthwhile to switch your advertising campaign's message from your product's benefits to emphasizing the potential for a wasted opportunity:
- *"Don't miss this chance..."*
- *"Here's what you'll miss out on..."*

Often, the product itself isn't all that important anymore. Alone the fact that the customer could lose a potential opportunity and miss out is reason enough for him to buy it. Sometimes people get so caught up in the deal or the negotiation that the reason why the want the product in the first place becomes secondary. They are just so focused on not losing the opportunity and that is all that consumes them.

The truth is that there will always be a new and better opportunity available in life. But if you have built up the client in your sales presentation so that he is most motivated to buy in that particular moment and then you potentially take away the opportunity for him to get it, he wants the product even more because of the fear of losing it.

Something new — people always want the new thing

In 1985, the beverage company Coca-Cola made their switch from their traditional formula to the sweeter formula "New Coke." Their taste tests indicated that 55% preferred the new Coke to the old.

Most of those tests were blind, but some participants were told which formula was new and which was the original. Under those conditions, the preference for new Coke increased by 18%.

> *When people know that they're getting something new, their desire for it will shoot up.*

What that 18% really meant was that when people know what it is they can't have, their desire for it will shoot up. Later, when the company replaced the traditional recipe with the new one, it was the old Coke that people couldn't have, and it became the favorite again. So make sure that you always include the word "new" in your marketing materials. People always want the new thing.

Getting a deal

> *People love getting a deal (or save money).*

Most people go crazy over a sale. If a product is 50% off, then they feel like they are getting a great deal. They feel like they only pay half for it. They are looking for opportunities to save money. They hate paying too much and getting something cheaper makes them feel great. Simply to put the words "sale", "50% off" or "clearance" in your offer and people will be motivated to buy it. It is possible that the product might have been overpriced to start with. But when you mark it down, people will perceive it as a deal.

If you sell a dress that normally sells for $1000 and then you mark it 50% off, people will think it is a great deal. But $500 might actually still be overpriced for that dress. Interestingly, most people only see the savings and then they ignore the rest.

The terms "savings" or "you can save X amount of dollars" will motivate most people. But the word "saving" is misleading. In reality you spend money when you buy something.

You don't actually save any money. You spend it. But if you put the word "save" in the right context and make it look like people need it anyway, then they "save money" compared to buying a more expensive product. It is all simply a matter of perception or point of view.

People love getting a deal. Any kind of price is always a perception in relation to the value that someone is getting in return. So if the customer perceives getting a higher value for the price that he pays, he will be motivated to buy the product.

> **So make sure that you position the value in such a way that it appears to be greater than the price.**

Once you have done that, mark it down or give an additional rebate. This will motivate someone even more to buy the product.

Sometimes, the last step of pushing someone over the edge so that he will order a product is giving a rebate in the end. Someone might be indecivise up to the very end but by turing the transaction into a deal for him, you can get him to agree to buy the product.

Comparison and contrast

The price of a product is always relative. It is always the perception of what you are getting in return for your money.

This is especially true when it comes to comparing a more expensive product with a cheaper product. The contrast principle works like this: You first mention a product that is much more expensive. When you then present a second product in comparison that is much cheaper, it will appear to be a great deal. Alone the comparison will help for someone to see it as a great deal.

Example: the competition's product costs $2000. Your company's product costs only $950. Compared to the most expensive product from your competitor, it appears much cheaper.

The same is true for any kind of comparison. You can use the contrast principle also in other areas to help to sell a product.

Example: the competitor will sell you ONE suitcase for $100. But your company will sell you a bigger-sized suitcase, a smaller suitcase, a carry-on case for an airplane trip and a personal handbag for $100. Compared to the competition you will get 4 items compared to just 1.

Another way is to take the whole world of 6.5 billion people and then compare them to a smaller number of people or even to one single person.

First example: there are six and half billion people in the world and half of them are connected to the Internet. Just because 20 people have a different opinion about this product, it doesn't mean that the other 3 billion people minus 20 people will not like it.

Second example: there are six and half billion people in the world and half of them are female. Just because one woman broke your heart doesn't mean that there are not enough other women out there who would be super happy to have you in their lives.

Making a comparison with a higher number will change the way you think about it.

> **You can influence other people by giving them a different point of view by comparing it with something greater.**

You can exaggerate it with extreme example so change someone's perception. Sometimes it is the only way to change someone's opinion about a subject or product. You can use the same information but change the message 100% by making comparisons.

First example: there are 300 million people is the US and 50 million of them don't have healthcare. That is really unacceptable for a first world country like this.

Second example: over 250 million people in the US have health insurance. That's basically everybody. The ones who are not insured are supported by social services.

You are using the same fact but how you present it will change the perception.

Time pressure

> **The longer someone is waiting to make a decision, the less likely will he do it.**

If you don't use time pressure, people will not buy your product.

If the customers feel like they have all the time in the world and can buy it later, they will see no reason why they must act now.

Time pressure will help to sell your product. If you tell them that the product will be gone or no longer available, they will feel like they might potentially miss out on an opportunity. By giving them a timelime they will feel the pressure to act before that timeline is up. If you tell them that the price will go up if they don't act now, they are more likely to buy now if they are on the fence. People need to have a pressure to act now (or soon) otherwise they will lose the motivation to buy in the first place.

The more time goes by between a sales presentation and the actual time of signing the contract, the less likely will a sale occur. When you make a sales presentation and motivate a client with all the good arguments but then give him time to make his decision, he will have forgotten most of the positive aspects of the product. One day later he will only remember half and one week later only about 10%.

The longer he waits, the more he will forget about the product and its positive features. You need to build up the customer's motivation to a high so that he is super excited. If he is still unsure or hesitant, then the use of a time pressure will do the trick.

"You must act now or the opportunity is gone." People hate to miss out and later regret not having bought the product. The also hate to pay more later if they don't decide now. The psychological pressure of having to make a decision now will become much stronger than reason. Often, it is the driving force behind making a buying decision.

> **People don't want to lose the chance or opportunity. They buy it even if they don't need it. Getting it is more important than the product itself.**

The law of simplicity and clarity

> **Simple and clear is more effective than complicated.**

Most people understand things best if you explain them in a simple manner. The more complicated things appear to be the less likely will people go for it.

Most sales letters are being looked at quickly. Only 10% of all people will read every single word and detail. The rest will only focus on the main headlines.

Keep most of your sales and marketing material simple and clear. Give clear instructions of what the customer must do otherwise he will be confused and simply won't do it. Most people need to be told what they need to do. Your statements must be simple, clear and every twelve-year-old kid must understand the message. If you make it too complicated, the masses will not follow.

It is an art to take something complicated and to simplify it. The world is already complicated enough. The more simple and clear you can explain something; the more likely your message will be effective.

Reciprocation

> *Give something first and then your client will feel obligated to do something for you.*

Reciprocation recognizes that people feel indebted to those who do something for them or give them a gift. The trick is to give someone a gift first. You can give free samples, a free report, free information, a free drink, etc. Whatever you do, it should give a positive experience to people and they will want to give you something in return.

Emotionally, people feel indebted to you if you do something for them first. They have the need to reciprocate the favor. Basically, you give them something and if they didn't give you something back, they are going to feel bad or rude. Most of us a simply programmed this way. We were raised to say thank you after we were given something.

But studies have also shown that people a more likely to donate to a cause or tip a waitress more money if they were given an unexpected gift. The gifts do not have to be expensive or even material; information and favors can work. This principle works really well in sales. If you do something for your client first, he will feel more obligated to buy your product.

Most carpet salesmen will lure you into their store by offering you a free drink or tea. Once you were given the drink and you are already in the store, they start showing you their selection of carpets.

Now, since you were given a free drink first, you are most likely to look at the carpets because you don't want to be rude. But once you start "looking", they will use every persuasion technique so that you will end up buying a carpet – even if you didn't really need one in the first place.

Social Proof

*If others have bought the product,
then new clients are more likely to buy it, too.*

Social proof is another factor that influences people greatly. When people can see that many other have bought the same product then they are more likely to trust it and buy it, too. Most people are afraid of making a wrong buying decision. If the masses or simply other people have bought the same product, then they can trust the company.

When people are uncertain about a course of action, they tend to look to those around them to guide their decisions and actions. They especially want to know what everyone else is doing. Testimonials from satisfied customers are another great way to provide social proof. They are even more effective with a picture. Especially, when the customers are similar looking or have a similar job that the person giving the testimonial. They will be more likely to become customers themselves in that case.

Most people work the same way on the inside and most people prefer things that are similar to them. If a lot of similar people have done it, then it can't be bad.

Often, hiring a celebrity to market your products can greatly increase the chances of selling more products. People will connect the positive feelings that they have from the celebrity with your product. They think that if he or she is behind this company then it can't be a bad company.

If someone refers a company or a person it can have a big influence and 50% of the trust level is already established. Most people are afraid of making a mistake and looking like a dummy afterwards. People are afraid to pay too much for a product or buy something that they can't return, has no follow up service or is not really fitting for them.

> *You need to take away the fear and risk from the client. Offer solutions with a money back guarantee. People are willing to pay more for a product if they have less risk associated with the purchase.*

Commitment and Consistency

> *People don't like radical changes.*

Most people don't like change. The older we get, the more we value consistency. And that makes it harder for older people to make a change. A recent study confirmed the belief that older people become "set in their ways."

In order to convince people you should praise them for making good past decisions, based on the information they had at the time. Then find ways to stress the consistent values connecting old actions and purchases with values underlying any new actions or purchases. People like commitment and consistency. People want to be both consistent and true to their word.

People do not like to back out of deals. We're more likely to do something after we've agreed to it verbally or in writing.

Liking

> *You can only sell to a person who likes you.*
> *Otherwise there is no sale possible.*

The main factor of selling any product to anybody is likeabilty. If the customer doesn't like the sales person, then he will not be able to sell the product. The way a sales persons looks is also important. The way he dresses, his smile, the way he talks, etc. Everything counts and a first impression is very important.

People are also more likely to favor those who are physically attractive, similar to them, or who give them compliments. Even something as random as having the same name as your prospects can increase your chances of making a sale. People like the same kind of people that are similar to them. If you are going to sell to a farmer in a dark suit and tie, then you are better off changing your clothes before you meet him. You are too different from him and that will lessen your chances.

Before you start any kind of sales presentation you should make sure that you work the first few minutes on developing a mutual basis for likeabilty. You need to ask questions and show honest interest in the other person. You should smile and be courteous. You clothes should be impeccable and your language should convey trust. You need to be open and likable so that people will like you back.

You can also only sell to a person if you have developed a good relationship first. Working and developing the personal relationship is key in any sales situation. Studies have shown that criminals who look good will get far less of a punishment.

When it comes to hiring people for a job and there are two people with the same qualifications, then often the person who looks better and who is more likeable will get the job. What can you do to improve how you look? Could you smile more? Could you dress better?

Authority

> *You need to position yourself as an expert.*
> *You will be much more successful this way.*

People respect authority. They want to follow the lead of real experts. Business titles, impressive clothing, and even driving an expensive, high-performing automobile are proven factors in lending credibility to any individual. Giving the appearance of authority actually increases the likelihood that others will comply with requests – even if their authority is illegitimate.

When people are uncertain, they look outside themselves for information to guide their decisions. Given the incredible influence of authority figures, it would be wise to incorporate testimonials from legitimate, recognized authorities to help persuade prospects to respond or make purchases.

It is better to position yourself as a real expert than a person who can do almost anything. People prefer experts.

Gaining pleasure or avoding pain

> *People are motivated by gaining pleasure or avoiding pain.*

Humans have two basic motivations: gaining pleasure or avoiding pain. Almost everything that we do is based on those two principles.

When it comes to selling you should not only motivate your client with the potential gains and profits. Often, the motivation of avoiding pain or loss is the much stronger motivational factor of the two.

Sometimes it can be even very powerful to "put fear into the client". Sometimes mentioning a small detail or describing a situation in such a way that the client could potentially be in a really bad position is all you need to do in order to convince someone. The motivation to avoid that potentially bad situation is enough for him to buy your product. A good example is life insurance. If you simply describe the potential outcome without having the insurance and painting a really dark and sad picture, you can motivate your client to buy the policy.

> **Most people are driven by fear.**

After 9/11 the government implemented a lot of new airport security rules. Most of them are really annoying and often lack common sense. But people accept them because the media and the government put a lot of fear into them.

Trying to avoid a bad situation is a great motivator. If you describe the situation in detail and use a lot of emotion you will be able to motivate the client to buy your product.

Ego, prestige, pride and comparison with others

> **"Vanity is great motivation, to be fair."**
> (Matthew McConaughey)

At first, most people are "not interested" in your products. Most people are swamped with sales offers. A lot of people are making their buying decisions based on "how they feel" right in the moment.

People are motived to buy when they have the feeling that they will get more money in the future, have fewer costs or if it makes things easier or more convenient. They also buy things if it makes things faster, more beautiful or if it increases their social status (comparision with others, ego-oriented).

A lot of people suffer from an inferiority complex and they will do anything to feel superior to others. 90% of people are jealous and envious of others because of lack of self-confidence. If they can buy a product that helps them to feel better in comparison to others, it can be a very strong motivation.

Most people want:
- More money
- Speed
- Lower costs
- Beauty
- Ease and convenience
- Ego, status and recognition

Your product should always include and focus on achieving one of these things.

A lot of people are a driven by brand names or even intangibles things that increase their social status.

Some people are driven to obtain scarce goods or products that are rare just because it makes them feel special.

People have the need to feel special or superior to others. They are driven by recognition and lack of love. They think that they will be able to get more recognition, attention and love by having something special that other people don't have.

Some people are so strongly driven by prestige and recognition that almost everything they do is based on that motivation.

Relationship based selling

> *You need to focus on the personal relationship with your client if you want to be successful.*

Clients have changed in recent years. They are ar much better informed and they demand a higher level of service. The competition is much better than in the old days and there are more products available than ever before. 20 or 30 years ago people used high pressure selling techniques to get people to buy their products. This type of selling style is long obsolete and doesn't work anymore.

If you focus on building a personal relationship, then the product will sell. You should focus about 40% on building trust, 30% of developing a need, 20% on your actual sales presentation and 10% for the closing.

> *Listening and asking questions will increase the level of trust.*

There is a thing called the friendship factor. A person will not buy from you if they are not convinced that you are their friend and that you act in his best interest. A top sales people are experts in building relationships. Even if you sell products online you have to focus on trust. Most people are very skeptical and don't believe you if you present a typical BS story. Your story must be real and believable.

Credibility

> *You need to have credibility to make a sale.*

Most people are scared of making a wrong buying decision. They are worried that they make a mistake, pay too much for a product or look bad in front of their friends.

Everything that you do as a sales person will either increase your credibility or it will lessen it. The first impression accounts for 95%. The way you dress, how you look, your attitude, smile, how you talk and present yourself are key in the beginning when you meet a new client.

But it also matters what the reputation of your company is. How long is your company in business? How many clients does it have? Where is it the market leader? What is its market share? All those factors will increase credibility.

The same is true for your marketing material. If your brochures and business cards look cheap or unprofessional it will damage your credibility. So remember: every little detail counts!

Creating a problem or deficit first to develop a need

> *Make someone aware of a problem first and then he will develop the need to do something about it.*

If you play a wrong tune on the piano, please start to cringe. It feels wrong and people feel uncomfortable. But people will relax again once you continue to play the right melody. The same is true when it comes to selling.

Sometimes you need to make your client aware of a situation that is wrong. Once you describe in detail how bad a situation is, he will develop the need to change it. Example: a person is happy and careless when you meet him. He is content with his life and doesn't worry about anything. Now you talk about starving children in the world. You show him pictures and tell him how bad their nutrition is and that a lot of children suffer from hunger. You go into a lot of details and your client will start to feel more and more unconfortable.

He will start to feel guilty that he has everything and those children have nothing.

Now you ask him to donate money for your cause. If you went under his skin it is almost impossible for him to say no because he feels so bad. By letting him sign up for your donation program, he will feel better about himself.

In general, you need to create a problem situation or deficit in any sales situation so that the client will develop the need or motivation to want to change it. Your product must be the solution to that problem.

You can also make people aware of problem that they are currently not aware of. This could be a problem with the IRS (US tax department), losing money or interest in your bank or by not having any money for retirement. People often don't think about those kinds of problems and therefore they don't have the need to do something about it unless you make them aware of it.

Choosing the right words matters

Choosing the right words can make all the difference.

Words have the power to start wars and to end life. The way you chose your words does matter greatly. Words have a much stronger influence on our emotions, perceptions and attitudes than we are aware of. Words create emotions and make us do things. That is why it is crucial HOW you say things. The way you say it will be a huge determining factor in any situation – sales or personal.

When it comes to a life insurance premium for example, you could use the word "pay" or the word "save". We associate paying with paying bills and it is negative. But saving for retirement is a good thing. Basically, it is the same thing because the action and the result are the same but the client feels better about saving than about paying.

Sometimes it also helps to use words that will scare the client in losing something and because of that he is motivated to do the opposite. It often only takes one word or one expression that will emotionally trigger the client to buy your product.

It could be as simple as: *"And you don't want to be dealing with the IRS because of not doing it properly, do you?"*

The potential fear of having to deal with a problem in the future might be all you need to convince a client.

Curiosity

> **The most curious animal in the world is not the cat — it's the human.**

Most new sales people make the mistake that they focus too much on the product and its features and that they come out with everything right from the start.

People are curious and it is a very strong feature that drives them. You can explain everything about the benefits of your product but you should wait for as long as you can before you present them with the solution. The client must first really feel it and be convinced that he needs it.

You should constantly building up curiosity so that people give you 100% of their attention.

When you make a phone call, you need to add a sentence that will make them curious so that they will follow up with the appointment. When you first meet them you can reveal some things but not everything. Only when you feel that the client is ready then you can show him everything. But in selling you need to build up his motivation and you can do that best by using curiosity.

The law of associations

> *People will associate positive emotions with past experiences.*
> *Connect those with your product and you will sell your product.*

Symbols, music, smells or other things will create associations in people. Often we connect and associate those things with positive events or memories. This will give them positive and happy feelings in return.

Americans are very proud of their country, for example. The symbol of the bald eagle is connected with the values of freedom, independence and pride. If your company has the symbol of the bald eagle in its logo, you will subconcisouly address those emotions in people.

People connect positive experiences and emotions from the past with certain things. If you can find out what a person feels very strongly about (a hobby, a person, an event, etc.) and you can connect that with your product in a positive way, you will easily be able to sell your product.

But also colors matter. Dark blue for example conveys trust. So if a sales person wears a dark blue suit and talks about money, he will automatically be perceived as more trustworthy. If he wore a yellow suit with bright green stripes, that would not be the case.

The law of involvement

> *Once you have one foot in the door, the sale is half done.*

Let your client have a free sample without any obligations. Let him enjoy a product and let him feel how much better his life is with your product. Car salesmen know this trick well.

They let you have the brand new car for a day without any obligation. Once you drive around in a brand new car with the new car smell and the beautiful new inside, it will be hard for you to return the car afterwards and go back to your old beat up car.

People are lazy and if they have to reverse a new and better situation it will be painful for them. And because of that reason people will keep the product. Once you can get your client involved by asking him only to sit down with you for 10 minutes, you have him on the hook. 10 minutes sounds realtivly risk-free but once you start your sales presentation it will be hard for your client to get up and leave. People don't want to be rude and they will continue to listen to you even if it takes more than 10 minutes. But once they are made curious and see advantages, they are likely to buy your products.

Sometimes all you need is an opening. The rest will take care of it own. Some sales people are so good once they get the chance that they can draw from their arsenal of tricks so that they client has no chance anymore.

The law of balance

95% of all buying decisions are made on an emotional level.

Even though most decisions are made on an emotional level, you also need to talk to the left side of the brain and give reasons, facts and figures.

Everybody is afraid of making bad buying decisions. That is why you must give him examples, assurances, statistics or statements from experts to help him to lose the fear.

Every product has advantages but also disadvantages. That is why you must bring up objections yourself and then answer those objections in your presentation.

Sooner or later your client will ask about some of the negative features of your product anyway but if you can be in control over how it is being presented and how you can make it look, chances are that they will not be perceived as negative by your client as if he brought them up.

Talking about negative features in the beginning will also increase your level of trust. You appear to be more honest and that is why the client will trust you more.

> **It is best to take objections away from the start**
> **so that the client can't bring them up later.**

It is your job to help your client with his buying decision. You must be aware that he will make his decision based on emotions but you also must give him some facts and details to make him feel goob about the purchase.

CHAPTER 3

IMPROVING YOUR **COMMUNICATION** SKILLS

Communication is everything

Communication is the key to personal and career success.

Everything that we want to achieve in life whether it is personal or professional has to do with some sort of communication. That is why it is important to learn to communicate exceptionally well so that you can achieve all your goals. The most famous people are successful because they have learned to present themselves in the best possible way and because they can communicate better than others. The better you can communicate the better will be the quality of your life. Communication is everything.

In school, kids learn algebra and calculus but they ought to learn communication skills. Knowing how to communicate can make all the difference between a good life and a bad life. In extreme cases it can decide if someone lives or dies.

We are not just in the information age. We are actually in the communication age. Social media and the Internet are tools for communication. But during the interaction with people face to face you must learn how to communicate properly. It is the most important human skill there is. It will make all the difference in your paycheck and in your personal relationships.

Let's make some examples: if you take two football players who have the same level of skill on the field playing football but one of them gives lots of interviews and autographs, he will automatically be more popular and therefore will make more money. He will get more promotional deals and his value to get traded to another team will increase. (If you don't believe me just watch Jerry Maguire with Tom Cruise...)

Two politicians may have the same plans but people will vote for the one who can communicate better. They will vote for the one who has the better rhetoric. If he can "beat" the opponent in a debate with better communication skills and techniques, he will get elected – regardless of his political strategy.

Sometimes little things like the facial expressions, the intonation, and the speed or the volume of the voice will be a major decision factor. Sometimes one word too much, the wrong reaction, being too serious or the wrong answer can completely change the outcome.

> **WHAT you say counts. But HOW you say it counts even more.**

If someone called you and said to you: "I would like to meet with you. It is about a lot of money. Are you available tonight?" Would you most likely say yes? Probably. The same person could add: "We will meet on main street number 55." But if he said: "We will meet on main street number 55, right next to the prison", you might reconsider, right?

Just by adding this last part your whole mood and motivation will change. You will probably have some negative associations when it comes to the word prison.

It also makes a huge difference how you communicate with a woman for example. You could say something like: "Every time I look into your eyes, I start dreaming of you." Or instead you could say: "Every time I look into your eyes, I lose my mind because of you." You would probably get a kiss for the first sentence and a slap in the face for the second one.

> **How we communicate and how we say things matters very much. But it also matters WHERE we say things.**

If you are in a public bathroom standing at the urinal with someone and you want to convince him to invest his money with you, it won't be a good time and place.

YOUR OUTFIT is also important. If you just changed the oil on your car and you are in your blue overall suit from the garage and you want to convince someone to make an investment, then the outfit doesn't match what comes out of your mouth.

Even changing a couple of words around in a sentence can make all the difference.

Two religious people are asking the main priest for permission to smoke during prayer time. The first one asks: "Can I smoke during my prayer?" The answer will probably be no. The second one asks: "Is it permitted for me to pray while I smoke?" The answer in that case will most likely be yes.

As you can see, language matters so much.

YOUR ENERGY about a subject is also relevant. It is hard to say no to someone who is happy and smiling when asking a question. Can you really say no to a child who is excited and jumping up and down asking for an ice cream after dinner?

Two people convicted for the same crime will get a different kind of punishment based on how they LOOK and how they communicate. The good looking person will get less of a punishment than the one who has a typical face of a criminal. Studies have proven this fact.

Learn the three basics rules of communication and interaction

Communication is a skill that you can learn.
It's like riding a bicycle or typing. If you are willing to work at it,
you can rapidly improve the quality of every part of your life.

There are three basic rules when you are dealing with other people:
1. Avoid criticism and judgment
2. Give lots of praise and recognition
3. Encourage and motivate others

No one likes to be around people who are constantly negative or criticizing everything and everybody. People who criticize others will eventually be alone in life. No one likes criticism. Even if you win with an argument by being critical and righteous, you will lose the person.

A saying goes: *"Laugh and the world will laugh with you. But cry and you cry alone."* People who are negative, cynical or critical will never amount to very much in life.

People who constantly have the need to criticize others are unhappy people and all they are doing to do put others down because they can't handle their own imperfections. Great people don't criticize others. They lift others up.

We live in a society where people don't get enough praise and recognition. Everybody loves praise and recognition.

> **Most people don't feel appreciated and loved.**
> **They are basically starving for attention.**

Once you have really understood this fact you can use it to make others feel better. If there is something positive that you can say to someone, do it. The reward you will get in return will be much greater.

People will like you immediately if you say something positive about them. It is very simple, Psychology 101, and it doesn't hurt you or cost you anything to say something nice about someone else.

Always ask people about their goals in life and their aspirations. Show some honest interest in the other person's life. Motivate and encourage other people to go for their dreams. Tell them how much you support their ideas and plans. Encourage them to live for their goals. See if you can help them in any way. Maybe you can give them a tip or a referral that will help them to get one step closer to their dream. Once you have helped or encouraged them, they will turn around and try to help you.

How to get other people to like you (building rapport and likeability)

Intelligence, knowledge or experience are important and might get you a job, but strong communication skills are what will get you promoted.

The best ways to get people to like you are:

1. Show an interest in other people
2. Be a happy and smiling person yourself
3. Use his / her first name often

4. Be a good listener
5. Talk about his / her interests
6. Increase his / her level of self-confidence

Show an honest interest in other people. Every person wants to be and feel important. If you show an interest in the other person, you will also get a lot more recognition yourself.

The idea is to ask the other person a lot of questions and not talking about you too much. Ask as many questions as possible about his work, his life or his hobbies. Let the other person talk more while you listen. You can have an entire conversation based on the things that you have asked him but you never actually said anything or much about yourself. The interesting thing is that he will later say that it was great talking to you and that you are a great person – even though you didn't say anything about yourself really.

The world is full of negative and unhappy people. If you smile, you will attract other people. Smiling and being happy is a very powerful tool. People can't help but to like you back if you smile a lot. No one is immune to someone who has a positive and happy energy. It is hard not to like someone like that. If you smile and laugh a lot you will be more attractive and appear more self-confident in the eyes of other people.

Use the other person's first name as much as possible.
The other person's name is the most important word for him or her.

Always repeat his or her name and if you have forgotten it, don't be afraid to ask for it again. Make it your new strength to remember first names. It is so much more important than you might imagine. If you can remember people's first names, they feel much more important and they will value you more, too.

Being a good listener is a key skill when it comes to communication. Always listen well and always ask a lot of questions to get more information from the other person. Be present and make eye contact when you listen. As a general rule, the other person should talk about 70% of the time and you should only talk about 30%.

If you want to win the other person you must talk about the things that interest him. Don't talk about yourself and your hobbies. Ask the other person about his interests. Ask a lot of questions and give lots of praise and recognition. Say things like: "Wow, that is very interesting. I have never thought of that or I have never heard that." People love to talk about themselves. It is the most important thing for them.

When you show interest in the other person he or she will return the favor sooner or later and start to show interest in what you do. People need praise and recognition to build their level of self-confidence. When you ask a lot of questions and show an interest in the other person, you should also give them lots of praise and recognition to encourage them in what they do.

Try to do whatever it takes to help to increase his level of self-confidence. If you help them and encourage them, they will always stand by your side and support you, too. You must first help them and later they will do what they can to reciprocate the favor.

How to win an argument and convince others

The only way to win an argument or a fight is to avoid it.

In an argument there are only losers. Every one wants to be right but people forget that they destroy the relationship by wanting to be right. It is often much better to avoid an argument altogether. Some people are so stuck in their opinion that it doesn't make sense to try to force them to accept your opinion in the moment. It is better to wait and try a different strategy or approach.

You first need to create a situation where the client is open to receive a new idea. You first need to acknowledge his point of view first, agree with him and then he will be much more likely to listen to what you have to say afterwards. You can then start with a hypothetical question to open up his mind.

Example:

His statement is: *"Your product is way too expensive and that is why I don't want it."*
Your response: *"You are absolutely right. I totally agree with you. If I were in your shoes I would say exactly the same. I can understand where you are coming from."*

Now at this point you have brought him from a negative position into a neutral position.

You continue: *"Assuming there was a good reason why the product is so much more expensive than the competitions' and it would actually save you money in the end, would you be willing to at least look at it to find out for yourself?"*

You just asked a hypothetical question to open him up for a new possibility or option. At this point his response is likely to be more open. He has made his point initially and now he is ready to listen to what you have to say.

You always need to respect the opinion of the other person and never say: "You are wrong!". If someone is convinced of his opinion but you know that he or she is wrong, then don't criticize him or her and make him feel bad.

Often a person with a strong opinion is missing an important piece of information to change his opinion. Therefore, you should tell him that he is right from a particular point of view but encourage him to see your side as well. Make sure that he never loses his face.

But in case that you are wrong, you must admit it immediately. Nothing is worse than fighting a fight that you cannot win because you are wrong and don't want to admit it. If you realize that you were wrong, admit it immediately so that the situation will be resolved quickly.

If there is hostility from the other person; you cannot fight back with even more hostility. Aggression will always provoke more aggression. Don't think you can win an argument by getting angry and loud. It doesn't work.

I once was waiting in line at the counter of an airline. The person in front of me was not happy because he wanted and demanded an upgrade to business class. He got so loud and angry with the person at the counter that it was almost embarrassing to watch. He acted like an angry little child who was stomping his feet. The longer it went on the worse it got and the person behind the desk was less likely to help him out. The woman behind the desk completely shut down and refused to give him service. I totally sided with her.

Now if he had tried to be courteous and friendly, maybe she could have done something for him. Maybe it would have been in her power to do something for him. But because she was treated with disrespect, he got the opposite result of what he really wanted.

You must always try it with friendliness when you want something from somebody.
If you want to achieve something, use common sense and most of all be friendly.

People who push and use anger will almost never get what they want.

If you are in a conflict you must always make the first step and meet the other person half way. Give others the opportunity to say "yes". You will only get a positive reaction from the other person if you make the first move. Be friendly first or apologize first so that the other person can meet you half way and doesn't have to lose their face. You don't need to be proud and stupid. If you want someone to do something you cannot expect the other person to act if you are being stubborn yourself.

In order for you to say the right things in a difficult situation and to get the other person to do what you want, you must first gather as much information as possible by letting the other person talk more. The more information you can get, the better you can use it to achieve your goals. You will know how to communicate better and what strategy to use. So let the other person talk most of the time.

Let the other person also believe that it was his idea.

> **If you want to convince someone of your idea or plan, you must slowly develop and build up the conversation in such a way that the conclusion seems to be coming from him.**

Sometimes it is difficult to understand and to accept an opinion from another person. Try to put yourself into his or her shoes and at least try to understand why he or she is thinking or acting that way. Try to honestly see his point of view. By doing that you will develop a lot more understanding which will have a positive result in your communication.

Always praise good intentions or positive suggestions. The more positive the mood and atmosphere is around you, the more positive inputs will come your way.

And finally, you must understand that deep down no one is a bad person. Even a criminal justifies his behavior. If you try to use common sense and encourage the other person to change his negative actions, he will be much more open to accept them. Encourage him to set a higher standard and nobler motives. You can say things like: *"Come one. This is not necessary. We can fix this a different way."*

If you want to win someone for your cause you must be able to inspire him or her. You must be excited and full of fire yourself first. The bigger the excitement is inside of you the more likely can you spark or ignite the excitement in the other person. If you want to sell your ideas you must describe them in a colorful way and be as positive and excited as you can be. You must be able to convince the other person by sparking the excitement.

You can also challenge the other person to do his or her best. Competition and challenges are often viewed as a positive form of motivation. It motivates people to get better.

How to change other people without offending them

If you want to change someone without offending him or her you should do the following things:

• You should always start with praise and recognition. Begin by praising the other person and his achievements and give honest appreciation.

• If the other person made a mistake you should never point it out directly. You should always do it indirectly if possible. You can talk about your own mistakes first before you criticize the other person. You should always give the other person a chance to save his face. You should always give him the opportunity to correct the problem on his own.

Let me give you an example: The CEO of a company would like his employees to clean up the coffee room because it is always messy. Instead of going into the coffee room and yelling at everybody, he could go in there when everyone is on their coffee break and in the same room. He could enter and start cleaning up. He could say something like: *"I really should clean up my dishes after I drink my coffee. The mess is all my fault."*

In reality, as the CEO, he should probably never have to clean up himself. But people see it and then they realize that they created the mess and that they should clean it up better in the future. He doesn't have to say anything. They will get it and understand it on their own. He can tell them indirectly that he expects the coffee room to be clean without having to criticize them directly.

> *Always begin with praise and honest appreciation.*
> *Call attention to people's mistakes indirectly and talk about*
> *your own mistakes before criticizing the other person.*

You can also ask questions instead of giving direct orders. Always make sure that the other person can save his or her face.

If you want someone to do more of a good behavior, you should praise even the slightest improvement and praise every improvement. People love praise and they want to get more of it. If you "catch" them when they do something right, give them more praise.

They will develop a habit of trying to impress you and doing more of the good things. Give people a fine reputation to live up to. Show them that you believe in them and that you value them so that they will continue to live up to that reputation.

Always use lots of encouragement. Make the fault seem easy to correct.

> **If someone made a mistake, don't beat him or her up over it.**
> **Play it down and say that it was no big deal.**

Your positive reaction will enable the other person to see that they can trust you even if things are bad. You don't need to tell someone that they have screwed up. They know it themselves already.

Making them feel worse is never helping the situation. Things can always go wrong and then you must quickly get back on track by staying positive in your communication. The wrong reaction could have negative consequences. Some people can't take criticism at all and in that case you would lose that person indefinitely.

Also make positive suggestions on how a problem could be fixed. Say things like: *"Don't you also think that this way would be a better way?"*

You can also use a story from your own past to show him what went wrong. By telling him a story about yourself or from someone else you can tell him indirectly how the behavior should be corrected.

> ### *If you make sure that people can save their face,*
> ### *they will thank you for it later.*

Also show the other person that you have a high opinion of him or her. And because of that he or she will tend to want to live up to that expectation. If you treat people as if they were already better, they tend to get better.

Encourage others to improve and change their behavior. Fact is that no one is free of mistakes and nobody is perfect. Let them feel that making mistake is no big deal and that it is easy to correct it.

Most people have low level of self-confidence as it is and by not hurting them even more emotionally, they will be thankful for it and even try to help you.

It should be a pleasure for the other person to help you with your desires. If you do something good for someone they tend to want to do something good for you, too.

A nice word or a small favor can go very far.

How to criticize the right way

> ### *Criticism is the biggest killer to someone's motivation*

If you are a jerk and criticize people constantly, you will not get the desired results out of other people. If you feel that you must dominate someone by putting them down, then you are in the wrong position or you have a personality problem.

Sometimes criticism or feedback is necessary BUT it is crucial HOW it is done.

Here are some rules:

• Always ask yourself what the goal of your criticism is. Do you really want to correct a behavior or do you want to show who is in charge because you feel that your authority has been challenged? Remember: You can win an argument but you can lose the person.

• Never criticize someone in front of other people. Criticism should only be done in private between you and the other person. Nothing can embarrass or destroy someone's self-worth more than being criticized in front of a group.

• If you criticize someone you should only criticize THE BEHAVIOR and NEVER THE PERSON. Don't say: *"You are a real idiot because you did that..."* Instead you should say that they action or behavior was unacceptable and never attack the person itself.

• Every criticism needs to be followed by a positive compliment and encouragement of better behavior. You could say: *"Your behavior was unacceptable. I expect more of a person of your caliber and personality. This is not typical for your standards. Normally, you are such a great person."*

Listening is a key skill

There is only one rule for being a good talker – learn to listen.

In a conversation, you should be listening 70% of the time and only talking and asking questions 30% of the time.

The more you listen the more information you can get from the other person. In order to communicate effectively in sales, you must be able to gather as much information as possible so that you can use that information to close a deal. You must know and understand what drives the other person and the only way to do that is by listening.

> **"The art of effective listening is essential to clear communication, and clear communication is necessary to management success."**
> (James Cash Penney – JC Penney)

Sometimes you can communicate by not saying a word at all. To communicate through silence is a link between the thoughts of man. Your facial expression and your body language can say so much without you having to say one word.

Being able to be silent in the right moment is a key skill, too. It is almost an art to use pauses effectively in a communication. If you can learn to make a pause at the right moment, you will create a lot more emotions in the other person. You can do it on purpose to get the other person to feel a certain way.

Sometimes it is better to be quiet than to talk. Talking is silver but silence is golden. But don't forget to listen when you are silent.

Asking questions is a key communication skill

> **The one who is asking the questions is always leading the conversation.**

We are conditioned to answer when being asked a question. It is considered rude not to answer. You can use that to your advantage.

Sometimes new sales people want to go through their planned sales script and too many questions from the client gets the whole flow interrupted. The presentation is upside down and is losing structure and direction.

Too many unwanted questions can ruin everything.

The key to deal with too many unwanted questions is to ask counter questions. Remember the main rule: The one who is asking the questions is always leading the conversation. You cannot give away the control over the conversation. You must always stay in charge of the direction and the content.

The more you practice question techniques, the better you will get at it.

Gentscher was German politician (chancellor) who said to a reporter that he has the right to ask him any question that he wants. But Gentscher also added that in that case he also has the right to give any kind of answer that he wants to give. Gentscher was known to never actually or precisely answer questions. He would simply talk about the topics that he wanted to talk about.

> *You are always in control of the conversation and the content. You don't have to answer exactly what you are being asked if you don't want to.*

But most people are so conditioned to give an answer when asked a question that you can use that conditioning to your advantage.

General instructions for a successful communication

If you are dealing with clients you should always follow these 10 basic rules and instructions:

1. Always be honest
2. Don't hide behind a company or a name
3. Tell the client more of what he wants to hear
4. Don't use pressure
5. Tackle his curiosity
6. Have the courage to ask anything

7. Be excited and positive
8. The client must like you and you must like the client
9. Show compassion and understanding for a problem
10. Communicate clearly

Always be honest and don't say any half-truths. Sooner or later these things will always come back to you in a negative way. Sometimes it is much better to say something negative in the beginning even if you have to risk losing the client or the deal. But often people will value your honesty and because of that they will trust you more.

> **When you communicate with other people you must be self-confident about yourself. Don't hide behind the name of your company.**

The client has a relationship with you and not with the company – even if it has a great reputation. Ask yourself what you would like to see or hear if you were a client. Put yourself in the client's shoes. What would you want to hear if you were the client?

Some people are coming on too strong. They use too much pressure and they are too slimy. They don't seem to understand or feel if they bother someone. In 99% of the cases, a client who feels uncomfortable will never buy anyway. People are more curious than cats. Don't give out too much information initially. Keep the curiosity at a high level. It is one oft he most powerful tools in your arsenal.

Have the courage to ask anything. And I mean anything at all. You need to know almost everything to in order to know how to proceed. If you smile and ask politely you can almost get away with anything.

The number one reason why people buy a product is because of the sales person and not the actual product. If you are enthusiastic and excited it will also excite the other person even if your product is average. The main thing is to work on the rapport and the relationship rather than just presenting a product. He will only buy a product if he likes you.

You must show compassion when dealing with a client. Listen to his problems and worries. Most people need someone that they can talk to and they are basically starving for someone that gives them attention. A lot people are lonely and they need human interaction. If you give him your time and attention, he will thank you for it.

How to win friends and influence people

Every successful person is automatically a great communicator. Once you have learned to communicate well you will always be successful.

The greatest book on communication *"How to win friends and influence people"* was written by Dale Carnegie in the year 1936 and everything in it is still true for dealing with people today.

No matter if you want to be successful in business or in your private life, this book has changed my life and the lives of many others in a positive way. This book is the foundation for learning and understanding other people and how to best interact with them. This book has changed my life. It has changed how I interacted with my wife, my family member and people at work. If there was one book about communication that I would recommend for anyone to read, it is this one.

When are you in a business transaction trying to get a deal you are always dealing with a person. People can feel if your intentions are good and if you want to create a win-win situation for both parties involved.

The social component in any communication is the most important factor. You are always dealing with a human being first. All the techniques and rhetoric comes after. The relationship always comes first.

Relationship management and emotional intelligence

All successful people are without exception experts in building relationships.

In order to be successful in today's market you need to realize that the most important factor is your relationship with your clients. If you focus on the relationship, your product will sell. But if you put your focus on the product rather than the relationship, you won't get very far.

There is a thing called the friendship factor. A person will not buy from you if they are not convinced that you are a good friend and that you will act in his best interest. Before you can even talk about the product, you must ensure that you have built trust and a good relationship.

> **You can only sell to a person if you like that person**
> **and a person will only buy from you if they like you too.**

There are different types of intelligence. The most important kind for a sales person and a good communicator is emotional intelligence. A person who has high levels of emotional intelligence can feel what the clients' worries and emotions are. He is aware that the focus of every conversation must lie on building the relationship and that everything that he says will have an influence on the clients' reaction.

Someone with high levels of emotional intelligence will realize when the mood changes and then can react to the situation accordingly. He can feel the other person's energy and understands how they feel.

A person with enough emotional intelligence knows what to do and when to do it. He can sense when it is a good time and when it is a bad time to talk about a certain topic.

> **"The most important thing in communication is hearing what isn't said."**
> (Peter Drucker)

In the end, only people who are sensitive enough to feel other people will be successful. When a conversation is difficult, one wrong word or statement can kill a sale.

But it is also when sales people are clueless about their own blabbering when the client seems bored and emotional intelligence is needed. In that case you need to change your approach and start speaking more dynamically. Ask yourself what kind of influence your statements will have on the client. Will you offend him? Will it improve the mood? How will he feel about it? What can you say or do to positively improve the conversation?

> **Emotional intelligence can be trained and developed.**

The more sensitive you get and the more you can find out how it made someone else feel when you asked a question, the more will you be able to change your approach and chose your language wisely.

Example of negative influence by creating negative associations

Language is very powerful. The kind of words that we choose will create or trigger certain associations. They can be used in a positive or in a negative manner.

Let me give you an example: in order to scare your kids and keep them from smoking cigarettes, you can tell them an emotional story.

You can tell them that you once had a friend who started to smoke at the age of 13. One year later he moved from smoking regular cigarettes to smoking joints (marihuana). A couple years later he started using hard-core drugs like heroin. He ended up homeless and living on the street. He lost everything and got really skinny. There were no more veins that he could use to set the syringe. His entire body was falling apart and he got really sick. Because he needed money for his drugs, he started stealing and cheating his friends. Everybody started to hate him and finally he killed himself with an overdose. And it all started with smoking cigarettes! So don't even think about starting to smoke because it will ruin your life and eventually kill you!

This series of negative emotions and pictures are very visual. The entire story is extremely emotional and has a lot of negative associations.

Obviously, the goal was to combine smoking with a lot of negative associations to prevent his kids from ever smoking again.

> ### Saying the right things will provoke emotions in the other person – positive or negative emotions.

Language can change everything. Hitler was a great communicator but a horrible person. He was able to control millions of people with his speeches and his communication skills. Communication can be very powerful and it can be used for good or bad purposes.

> ### Words are singularly the most powerful force available to humanity.

We can choose to use this force constructively with words of encouragement, or destructively using words of despair. Words have energy and power with the ability to help, to heal, to hinder, to hurt, to harm, to humiliate and to humble.

Words, so innocent and powerless as they are, as standing in a dictionary, how potent for good and evil they become in the hands of one who knows how to combine them.

> ### You can change your world by changing your words.

Remember, death and life are in the power of the tongue. The basic tool for the manipulation of reality is the manipulation of words. If you can control the meaning of words, you can control the people who must use the words.

Sending information to the receiver on a non-verbal level

> **When two people communicate with each other only 5% happens on a verbal level and the other 95% are non-verbal.**

When you communicate you are sending out signals. If the other person gets a bad feeling he or she will not trust you. The problem is not necessarily what you do or say, it is the other person's sub-conscious that will determine whether or not they trust you.

Imagine that each one of us carries a big old Neanderthal on our backs. The Neanderthal represents our sub-conscious mind. The Neanderthal is much bigger and stronger than we are and he is the real decision maker. But the Neanderthal is very dumb and only uses his emotions to decide whether he can trust you or not. It doesn't matter what you say because he can't logically understand it anyway. But it matter how you say it and if you are able to generate a feeling of trust.

If you can't win the trust of the Neanderthal then you have lost. It doesn't even matter how great your logical arguments are. So the main goal so to speak is to win the trust of the other person's Neanderthal.

Building rapport with NLP (mirroring) and building trust

NLP stands for Neuro Linguistic Programing. It is a series of psychological techniques that were discovered by Richard Bandler and John Grinder to improve communication between people.

One of the main techniques is called mirroring. It basically says that if you use the same body language, the same speed, and the same volume and breathe the same way as the person sitting opposite of you, he will feel more connected to you.

> **As humans we perceive and like people more that are similar to us. So if we have someone in front of us who is similar in his body language and behavior, we tend to like and trust that person more.**

The more you change your own body language and voice to match the person sitting opposite of you, the more he will like and trust you.

The same is true when you are prospecting on the phone. You should talk faster if the other person talks fast and you should talk slower if the other person talks slower.

In general, you will create rapport by smiling. Usually, the first five minutes are key when building rapport. Typically, you should not get into a sales presentation right away but use the first few minutes to do small talk. You should focus on the relationship and ask him questions about his life, work or hobbies. You can talk about sports or the weather.

In order to build trust there are a few factors that count:

1. Fist impression (smile, clothes, general look)
2. Character (integrity)
3. Competence (Knowledge)
4. Self-confidence
5. Credibility (Experience and history)
6. Congruence (consistency)

Like it or not but how you look will determine whether someone will like you and trust you. In order to make a good first impression you need to smile and be impeccable in the way you dress, how your hair is and how healthy you look in general. You can't expect people to trust you if you look like a bum from the street.

Your character, competence and self-confidence level are also indicators of how you are being perceived. Whatever you say and how you say it matters a lot. The way you speak and how well you can communicate will determine whether people will trust you.

There is one technique that I recommend doing. Typically, you should focus the majority of the conversation on the relationship with the client. But sometimes you must also prove that you are an expert.

What you do is to explain something technical for 5 minutes. It doesn't really matter if you client understands exactly what you are talking about but he just needs to get the feeling that you are an expert and that you know your field very well. This is a great way to build trust. Basically, what you do is to win over the Neanderthal.

As I mentioned, it is not important that he understands every technical detail of what you explain. It is important that in his head he goes: *"Wow, I don't really understand what he just said but I think he is a real expert... I think I can trust him...".*

> **Remember: everything counts! One small detail that is off and people will either have doubt or don't like you.**

In order to build trust it also matters what you do. Everything you do will either help your level of trust or diminish it.

Simplifying complicated things is great communication

> **Be smart and well educated but communicate in the language of the common people.**

Although you know your products inside out it is always the very first time that the client will hear your presentation. Try to be still excited about it and be very clear and precise in your communication. Explain it in such a way as if you were telling it to a 10-year child.

Make it very simple, understandable and logic in your approach. The more you know and the more complicated you present it, the harder it will be for your client to follow you. Try to focus on the very simple and basic ways of explaining something.

A big CEO always used the cleaning lady test. He said that before any big corporate announcement he would test his presentation and message with his cleaning lady. If she could not understand what it was all about he would have to make changes in the presentation and simplify it further. I don't want to imply that a cleaning lady has less intelligence. But often a cleaning lady does not have the same level of technical education like an MBA graduate. But when it comes to business it is important that you can understand the main message no matter what you educational level is.

Another way to explain something so that everyone gets it is to use the top-down approach. Basically, you start with the whole world, go into a specific country or region, then industry, then companies and finally you make your point. Example: there are a lot of oil companies in the world. Most of them are in North America – specifically in the US. When you look at the oil industry, the leaders are Exxon Mobil and Chevron. But there are dozens of smaller oil companies that will eventually become bigger. Company ABC oil is one of those companies. And we believe that it will be the new Exxon Mobil of the future. Here is why you should invest into it...

Respect and politeness

> *"You can say anything to me. But it matters how you say it.*
> *But if you get disrespectful or rude, it's over."*

Always show a lot of respect to the person you are dealing with. Most people feel like they are not respected enough. If you treat him better, he will return the favor and treat you better, too.

Everything that you do will either increase or decrease the level of trust and respect. In order to increase the level of trust you can say: *"Mr. Smith, if you were my own brother I would have to tell you now that...".* This statement can be very effective and powerful because you would never cheat your own brother in a business transaction.

Integrity and ethics are the basis for every business transaction. You should never compromise that. Always create a win-win situation for both parties.

The way you communicate is absolute key. Don't be aggressive, rude or insulting. You will not get very far like this.

Also, don't be a smart ass or cynical. If someone gets emotional with you, you should stay calm and your response should always be polite and rational. If someone gets overly rational with you and wants to give you a hard time about certain details, you should always counter with emotional statements.

Understand that people are different than you

> *"To effectively communicate, we must realize that we are all different in the way we perceive the world and use this understanding as a guide to our communication with others."*
> (Tony Robbins)

There are four different personality types: red, blue, green and yellow type. Each one of them describes the most common character traits of that type. Depending on how you are talking to you should adjust your own style. You need to understand how each type works, thinks and acts.

When you are talking to the red type you need to talk to him in a dynamic manner because the red type is mainly dominant, loud, dynamic and likes confrontation. The red type likes money, recognition, status and power. Red types love challenges and competition.

When it comes to the blue type the whole conversation is very rational and facts-oriented. You need to give him information, facts, statistics and numbers. The blue type loves to analyze things and go into detail.

The green type is very friendly and social. He constantly smiles and is very nice. When dealing with the green type you need to focus on the relationship. You need to be nice, friendly and talk about past stories. He loves to talk a lot and likes good company and friends.

The yellow type wants to be special and different from anybody else. He is usually very innovative and communicative. He likes public speaking and being creative. You can spot him because he always wants to be different and not follow the general norm.

> *There is no good or bad personality structure.*
> *Every personality structure has strengths and weaknesses.*

Most people have a dominant type and a secondary type. Based on the type that someone is you can find out what comes easier to that person and what doesn't.

But the sooner you know which personality type you are dealing with, the better you can adjust your own language to influence him or her. If you want to motivate someone you need to understand how he or she is wired. If you know how or with which tool you can motivate them, you will get further ahead. Here is again a summary of the main characteristics of each personality type:

- **Red type**

Impulsive, dominate, engaged, impatient, emotional, loud, active, dynamic, courageous, conflict ready, goal-oriented, prepared to take risks, will-strong, likes confrontation and challenges, demanding, restless, direct, likes adventure, alive, no patience.
Typical occupations: Sales person, pioneer, leadership role
Sports: Like racecar driver, fighter, and bungee jumping, individual sports

- **Blue type**

Detail-oriented, rational, precise, organized, systematic, steady, patient, reasonable, makes lots of plans, principle-faithfully, introverted, avoids physical contact, ironic, feelings are hardly recognizable, isolated, quiet, serious, on time, good with finances.

Typical occupations: Tax counsel, programmer, accountant, Computer specialist
Sports: Persistent kinds of sport, moving, running, chess

- **Green type**

Talkative, friendly, kind, makes others feel comfortable, ready to compromise, accommodating, likes to tell stories about the past, social, reassuring, open-hearted, emotional
Typical occupations: Social worker, kindergarten teacher, and customer service
Sports: Team player

- **Yellow type**

Innovative, artistic, communicative, unorthodox, versatile, spontaneous, flexible, surprising, tolerant, inspiring, superficial, influential, creative
Typical occupations: Artist, publicity man, speaker, and creative occupations
Sports: Mental games and exercises

It matters HOW you say it – choosing the right delivery

It matters greatly how you say something to someone. In every communication you have a goal. You either want to get something from the other person or communicate your thoughts.

If you want something from someone you must chose the right delivery. Some people (including myself) react really sensitive when you are being rude with them.

You can also get the exact opposite result of what you originally intended. If someone talks to me in an "order-like style" I will do the exact opposite because I hate orders. I am sure lots of people react the same way. Don't be a jerk about how to treat other people. You might have the "power" if you are the boss or if they need you but in reality you will never truly win over the person in the long run.

Some people are easily offended if you chose the wrong tone of voice. So be careful and apologize if you realize that you went too far.

> *You can be strong and true to yourself without being rude or loud.*

Dress for success

> *Clothes and manners do not make the man;*
> *but, when he is made, they greatly improve his appearance.*

The way you look is crucial when you are dealing with clients. Your success is dependent on your clothes, your hair and how well you take care of yourself.

I am sure you know the saying: *"Fine feathers make fine birds".*

In German we have a saying: *"Kleider machen Leute".* Translation: Clothes make people. Basically, it says that you can be anyone you want to be if you are just dressed the right way. If you want to be king, you must be dressed like a king. If you want to convey to be a successful businessman or financial advisor you must dress accordingly.

Make sure you chose your clothes well. You are not hurting yourself by being overdressed. Also make sure that you don't wear weird jewelry or armbands. Your hair should be impeccable and men should probably not wear earrings. Just make sure that no one says to you: *"Who picks your clothes – Stevie Wonder?"*

The way you dress will also influence how you feel and how you see yourself. It will also change how others perceive you and how they communicate with you. You will get a lot more respect if you are dressed like a rich and influential person than a person in jeans and a T-shirt.

One of my friends is very conscious about his dress code. He wears a suit every day even though he doesn't work in an office. He looks like a model CEO of a big company or bank.

But because he is dressed so well all the time we was able to deal better in certain problematic situations with other people because of how they perceived him. It has helped him countless times to get what he wanted. In real life he is just a regular telemarketer.

Mental attitude

1. Don't worry about rejection

2. Act with confidence and assume
   that the client wants to do the deal

3. Always act with empathy

4. Do more than is expected of you

When you are prospecting, you will get rejection. But that is normal and you should never take it personally. Most people are scared to being pushed into something that they will later regret. If your mental attitude is relaxed and you can be light-hearted and positive, your overall mood will not change negatively.

When you are dealing with a client you need to have his best interest at heart. Don't view him as a commission provider. He is a human being with emotions. When you feel that a situation is not right for the client you must change the situation. Sometimes it makes absolutely no sense and is a waste of time and energy to talk to someone who is not open to listen.

In the end you will only really win people over if you do more than is expected of you. Always try to find something where you can positively surprise them. This little effect can go very far. When you promise something, promise always a little bit less than you know you can deliver and then deliver more than you promised. This strategy is a key for long-term success.

Dealing with the opposite sex

The most important factor for a successful marriage is communication.

It also makes a difference how you talk to men or women. In general, women want men to listen to their problems but they don't want you to give them a solution. Men on the other hand always try to solve a problem and come up with a solution.

In order to improve the communication with a woman, a man should try to be quiet and just listen to what she has to say. Then he should acknowledge what she says and refrain from giving any solutions or advice. *(If men just did that alone, the world would be a better place. Ha, ha,..)*

Women on the other hand underestimate that men need a lot more praise and recognition. They want to hear that they are the best and that the woman thinks he is a superman. *(If women just did that alone... you know where I am getting at.)*

Women also communicate a lot more with body language than men. In a fight or disagreement they role their eyes, give a dirty look, cross their arms or give you the silent treatment. They also communicate in such a way that they say things that they don't really mean but just to let you know how much you hurt them. They want to hurt you with words so that you understand how they felt. Men are often at a loss for words and then they get frustrated. In some cases they get loud and angry because they feel that they cannot "win" the argument with a woman.

The key for men here is to read between the lines. Don't take every word literally. Take a step back from the situation and don't get so emotional. Try to understand what the real underlying problem is.

Often women don't communicate clearly what they want or expect. They get angry and don't explain why because they feel that men should know better. But the truth is often that men really don't know or understand what the problem is and that is why women must try to communicate very clearly and directly. They should say exactly what bothers them so that a man can realize it and do something about it.

Women should also watch out how they do their delivery. Often by getting angry or nagging they will actually achieve the opposite of what they intended. Men will take criticism very personal even if it was originally meant to help. A lot of misunderstandings can be prevented if people communicated better with each other.

> *The key to any successful relationship is communication. You must communicate what you want and how you feel. It can mean the difference in feeling happy or unhappy.*

The goal of a successful communication is to communicate effectively. This means that there are potentially a lot of misunderstandings when it comes to communication.

If, for example, a wife tells her husband to take out the garbage, it does not guarantee that he will actually do it. Just because she has said it to him does not necessarily mean that he has heard or understood it. Even if he has understood it, it does not mean that he agrees. And even if he agrees, it does not mean that he is ready to do it now or to keep doing it. So the general rule is this:

> *said ≠ heard ≠ understood ≠ agreed ≠ ready to do ≠ continue to do it*

Once you have understood this principle, your life will be much easier.

Asking your way to success

> *"Take advantage of every opportunity to practice your communication skills so that when important occasions arise, you will have the gift, the style, the sharpness, the clarity, and the emotions to affect other people."*
> (Jim Rohn)

People can speak 150 words per minute but they can understand up to 600 words per minute. If you want people's attention you should talk faster. If you are giving a presentation and you talk slowly it can easily get very boring.

When you are dealing with clients you should think about the questions in advance and prepare the answers. This will give you a lot more security and you will appear to be more professional. Top sales people also ask high quality questions to grab the client's attention and trigger emotions.

Some sales people ask questions and then give the answer themselves right away. Don't do that. Let the client speak. Only when he has a chance to really think it through and he gets it then you can continue. Remember also that just because he said yes that it automatically means that he will do the deal. Successful sales people use a lot of questions techniques to keep the control over the conversation. Learn everything there is to learn about question techniques and use a lot of questions with your clients. Questions are the key to a successful communication. I hope you were able to learn a lot of good lessons and this program will help you to achieve great success.

> *"Number one, cash is king... number two, communicate...*
> *number three, buy or bury the competition."*
> (Jack Welch)

CHAPTER 4

AMAZING
SALES
TECHNIQUES

Sales techniques in general

> *It is not good if someone can tell that you are using a sales technique. This will make the person feel like you are trying to trick him or her.*

A sales technique is only effective if no one can tell that you are using a technique. By using a sales technique you can influence the person you are talking to and you can create emotions and motivations that were not there before.

There are a number of sales techniques that are constantly being used in commercials, in ads or on television. Depending on the product that you are selling, you can use very obvious and simple techniques that will make a person with an average or below average intelligence buy your products. Some of them are even so obvious that everybody is aware of them but in the end they still buy the products.

Now, the key is to master certain techniques that are very effective and that can bring you the desired result but that are not obvious to detect.

Often, people just feel like the sales person is such a great person and because of that they bought the product. But in reality it was a number of well placed sales techniques that lead to the sale.

In order to influence someone with an above average intelligence you also need to create a situation where it is in the best interest of the other person to buy a certain product.

You cannot just trick someone into buying something that they don't need or that is not good for them. In the end it all needs to make sense, too.

But in order to become a better sales person, I have put together a number of techniques for you to learn so that you can increase your sales in your profession. I hope you will like them.

> *The sales techniques that you will learn in this program are not your every day typical sales techniques – they are for the advanced sales person and they are very powerful.*

Why am I qualified to talk about this subject?

I used to be the number one sales team leader in Europe of an organization with over 5000 employees. I have personally consulted over 3000 clients face-to-face and I have trained many sales people in my career. I have built several sales organizations and raised millions in capital for investments from clients.

I have written a book about sales psychology, which is a book based on my personal sales experience and success. I have earned millions of dollars with selling and I love selling.

I believe that everybody has certain talents that they were given in this life. Fixing a car or building a computer isn't certainly one of my talents – but sales and communication is!

Therefore I will teach you some of the best techniques and I hope that they will help you to achieve your personal goals and dreams.

Using metaphors

Most people understand things better if you are using a metaphor by giving a comparable example from another area in life.

Instead of saying that your product is a much better quality than the competition you could say that you have the Rolls Royce model of today and that the competition has the cheap Mazda from 1980. Or you could say that he can get there with a Ferrari or with a bicycle.

> **By making a comparison from another area
> it makes the point you want to make clearer.**

Metaphors are very powerful and sometimes by just giving one example, you have totally convinced your buyer and there is not much else that needs to be mentioned. You could also use a louder voice or body language to further emphasize your point.

Another example is that you can tell your client that he is currently climbing a steep hill but with your product he could simply go trough the tunnel be on the other side in no time.

But this technique also works in real life situations.

There was once a man who has hesitant to marry his girlfriend. Even though he loved her, he could not get himself to make a marriage proposal. His long-time girlfriend grew more and more frustrated and unhappy over this situation.

Her boyfriend loved playing soccer in a local team but he was always on the bench waiting to get into the game. He was always very frustrated about not being able to play and being kept on the bench during a game. His girlfriend used that example to let him know how she really felt. She told him that she also felt like him being on the bench because he wouldn't marry her.

Once he heard this comparison, he realized what he was doing to her and only a few weeks later they got married. Typical examples from every day life can be very efficient tools that everybody understands and agrees with. Other examples of metaphors are:

- Eating in a 5 star hotel or at the hot dog stand down the street
- Walking a marathon uphill on foot or taking the helicopter to get there
- Madonna is performing or the local girl from the church choir
- This is the Cadillac version compared to the standard cheap car
- Lebanon is the Switzerland of the Middle East when it comes to banking (actually a true statement from about 20 years ago...)

Top down approach

When it comes to mutual fund investment strategies there are two basic investment approaches: Bottom up and top down approach. The bottom up approach focuses on an individual company, compares it other companies in the region, compares it to the sector, then to the country, then the continent and finally the world markets as a whole.

The Top down approach starts with the world in general and tries to identify the best regions. Then it focuses on that region and its sectors. Once it has identified the best sectors it looks for the best companies in that sector. And finally it will choose the best company to make the investment.

> *You start with a general statement or the world as a whole.*
> *And then go down step by step into more detail until you arrive*
> *at the desired conclusion in such a manner that makes logical sense.*

When it comes to selling or explaining something logically, you can also use the top down approach. It is very effective because you start with a general question or statement. You can then logically explain by further going into detail why your product and company is the best choice. Let me give you an example:

- Mr. Client, you would like to find a good investment for your money right? Right.
- You would also like to make sure that you get the best return and that you are in an area that has growth potential, correct? Correct.
- Now when we look at the world of investments, I would recommend that we focus on North America. There are great opportunities in India, China, Russia, Africa and in Europe but in order to be on the safer side, I suggest that North America holds the best options, agreed? Agreed.
- Now within North America I would focus on natural resources because they do well when it the economy is shaky, ok? Ok.
- Within natural resources I would say that gold is the best investment because of this and that... Agreed? Agreed.

- When looking at a gold company we can chose between a old and long established player who is already overvalued or at a new and young exiting company with a lot of growth potential. Which one do you think is better? Young company with growth potential.
- That is why I recommend ABC Gold Company.

You went logically through all the factors and the conclusion was the company that you wanted to present. The client agreed to each step along the way and was following you and agreeing the whole time.

It was simply the logical choice and no other in the end what you were going to present to him.

> *You explained it to him in such a way that he almost thought that it was his ideaand his logical thinking that led to this choice.*

Had you started with the ABC Gold Company from the start you would have had a lot of explaining and defending to do.

Stories and emotions

> *95% of all buying decisions are made on an emotional level.*

Use words, stories and pictures that trigger emotions. If that weren't true, we would all drive a Toyota Prius. Apparently, the Prius has the best value to price ratio. But how many of us are actually driving a Toyota Prius? Certainly not me! Are you?

Most people want a car that gives them a certain feeling or emotion.

We are all driven by emotions and the more you are able to touch someone on an emotional level, the more successful you will be in selling your products. Most people are scared or worried and you need to make emotional statements or tell stories that go deeper.

> **Stories are a perfect tool for selling.**
> **Tell your client as many real life stories or examples as you can.**

We can all identify with stories and as kids we all loved our bedtime stories. They go emotionally deeper and we can relate to other people's stories.

The kinds of words that you use will influence people's emotions, perceptions or attitudes. Words create emotions and make people feel a certain way. That is why it is important HOW you say things.

Sometimes you need to use different words in your sales presentation to avoid negative associations. Instead of the word "pay" you can use the word "save".

> **It is basically the same action but the association is different.**

Instead of saying that you need to save for the next 40 years, which seems so far away, you could simply replace "40 years" with "long term horizon".

Symbols, music or smells will also trigger emotions or associations. People connect certain symbols with certain values. They can be positive or negative. Americans, for example, are very patriotic and the eagle is a symbol for freedom and independence. If your product has an eagle on the label, then people will associate those values and emotions with your product.

A negative description can also influence someone's emotional state and his motivation to take action.

If you are trying to sell a life insurance product and you tell your client that his wife and kids will have no money in the event of his death and that they have to eat dry bread, live in a dark one bedroom apartment with only one table and a rat is crawling across the floor because it is so cheap, then you will have created or painted a picture that is very emotional and that will get him to take action.

Answer all the questions first that he doesn't ask you but that are in his head anyway

At first, no one wants to buy your products and services. That is normal. We are all swamped with too many sales offers these days. But everybody who you get in contact with and who doesn't know you has some questions that you need to answer whether he will ask you or not. These are the questions:

1. Why should I listen to you?

2. What it is? What can it do?

3. Who else has bought it?

4. Who says so (except you)?

5. What is in it for me?

> **The goal is to communicate the value for the customer just like in "What is in it for me?" rather than the features of the product.**

Most people don't want to have big changes. They want to make sure that other people have also bought the product and that there are testimonials of happy clients, articles from newspapers and pictures. You need to give him proof and answer all those five questions in your opening statement.

People are driven by two main motivations:

1. To gain pleasure

2. To avoid pain.

Everything we do is based on these two principles. If we associate more positive emotions with a certain product, we are more likely to buy it. But if the product helps us to avoid pain, we are equally if not even more motivated to buy the product. A good sales person must create a lot of both kinds of emotions in his sales presentation by using statements and questions that trigger certain emotions.

> *In order for you to sell anything you need to create a motivation for him to buy. This motivation is a deficit or problem in his current situation. If you don't make him aware of that problem, he will not develop the motivation to buy anything.*

People are also more likely to buy from someone who is a specialist in his field or an authority. They tend to trust a person much more if they position themselves as an expert. So position yourself as an expert.

The contrast principle

> *The contrast principle compares a product with a normally higher price with a product that has a lower price. The perception from this comparison makes the lower priced product appear to be a great deal.*

The contrast principle is one of the most common and most used methods in selling. Typical statements go something like this: *"Normally this product costs $5,000 but today it is only $500!"*

Depending on the product $500 might still be a lot but if you put it in relation to $5,000 it appears to be a deal and cheap.

The contrast principle gives you the feeling like you are getting a deal. If the price of a product is $100 at first and you perceive it to be a lot of money but then you can get it for $50, you feel like it is cheap now and then you will buy it. Often, you will see this technique being used in infomercials. The price gets cut more and more the longer the infomercial is going on and in the end you will even get the twice the amount of the product for the lower price.

> **The contrast principle is all about perception. The product might still be overpriced but when put in comparison, it appears to be cheap.**

Some products are broken down to a fraction of the total amount. Things like "Just for a dollar a day" make it appear very affordable. And sometimes a bigger payment gets split up in 3 or 4 payments to make it seem lower. 4 payments of $24.95 sound a lot less than one big payment of $100.

Principle of assumption of deal

> **You should never ask a client if he wants to do the deal. You simply assume that he does and act accordingly.**

New sales people are still unsure about closing a deal and that is why they often ask the client if he wants to do the deal or not. By asking the client you still give him the opportunity to say "no" at the end.

A more experienced sales person doesn't ask. Based on a number of control questions during the sales presentation, he simply assumes that the client wants to do the deal and he doesn't ask him at all. He simply acts as if they client wants to do it and without hesitation he brings out the contract at the end of the presentation.

His whole behavior is in such a way that he simply assumes that the client wants it and he never asks him whether he wants to do it or not.

Because of this self-confident behavior most clients just go with it and do the deal.

If the client brings up an objection or some resistance, the sales person acts surprised and almost a bit angry because he cannot believe that the client will question his advice. This kind of behavior even if played or acted will often intimidate the client and he will no longer resist.

If you are selling a life insurance and you have explained all the advantages of the product then you could simply go into the closing phase by getting out the health questionnaire and start asking some health questions. If the client goes with it and answers them, you can assume that he will do the deal. In the end you simply say that he needs to confirm the validity of those questions and sign at the dotted line. Often, clients don't even realize that they just signed the contract because it all naturally flowed into each other. The sales person never asked the client if he wants to do it. He simply assumed the whole time that the client wants it and even needs to do it. There is never any doubt involved.

Taking the deal away from the client

People have a very special tendency
to want the things that they cannot have.

By taking away the deal from a client, some clients want it even more. Basically, you explain everything about your product to the client and give him all the positive advantages and you hold it right under his nose.

But when it comes to the end, you don't allow the client to close the deal. You take it away from him by making it very exclusive and you let your client know that he does not qualify for this deal.

If everybody can do it, no one wants it. If there is no value to a product, there is no special motivation for someone to get it. So if you don't make your product exclusive, you will not be able to close the deal. But if you make it special, there are some people who will do almost everything to get it. Often, it is a little bit dependent on the personality of your client how well this technique will work. Typically, you can say something like this:

You: *"Well Mr. Client, as you can see this product has a lot of advantages. But there is still one problem. Not everyone can get it and you must fulfill certain conditions to qualify."*

After this statement, you must stay quiet and not talk. Let him talk first. Typically, he will say:

Client: *"Why not? How can I qualify?"*
You: *"Well, I am not sure if you do. Therefore I must ask you a few more questions. But I am not sure if this product is really for you."*
Client: *"Oh, no please. Ask me. What do you need to know?"*

And in that moment you will have him 100%. He wants it badly.

This technique can be a bit provocative at times but works really well. Depending on the type of client, he will want your product more than anything in the world at that point in time.

Silence on purpose as a technique

At certain points during your presentation it is important to be quiet or silent and wait for the client to answer. Sometimes you can make a statement or ask a question that is very powerful and emotional and after you have said it you must be quiet.

> *You must let the client answer first and wait for as long as it takes.*
> *Whoever speaks first, loses.*

So therefore you must refrain from speaking when you apply this technique. Here are some examples:

Example 1:

- *Mr. Client, how much money did you earn with this investment last year? Nothing.*
- *And for how much longer do you want to tolerate this situation?* (SILENCE)

At this point you facial expression should say more than any words could. The client must feel that he needs to change something.

Example 2:

- *Mr. Client, each year you are paying $10,000 too much in tax. Do you think that is good? No.*
- *Should we change this?* (SILENCE)

The point is to make an emotional statement that goes under the client's skin. The few seconds of silence will create more emotions and they will make him understand that he needs to act. Most sales people lose a deal because they talk too much. Especially, once you have presented the client with an offer, you must shut up. Let it sink in. Give your client some time to realize what just happened.

> *Some sales people can hardly take the silence.*
> *They want to talk so badly and mention more things to get the*
> *approval. But key is the wait for him to speak first.*

Example 3:

If you are applying for a job and you ask for the range of the salary that you will get paid, the same principle applies.

Let's say that your future employer says that your salary will be between $80,000 and $90,000. He will give you this number because he has already thought about it before. He might even be able to go up to $100,000 if necessary but he mentions a lower range at first.

As the person applying for the job, you could take this range and then say *"$90,000, eh?"* and then be quiet. You take the higher number of that range and then wait until the employer speaks. If he offers you a range, he is very likely to hire you anyway. By being quiet at this point and waiting for the employer to speak, he might not be able to take the silence and even through in a few more benefits so that you will say "yes". He might even say that he could go up to $100,000 and give away all his aces.

> ## So remember: the person, who speaks first, loses.

Making a bold statement or claim

If you make a claim whether it is true or not but you present it with conviction, people will accept it as truth. This technique is very popular with politicians. They make a statement or a claim that no one can really prove not to be true.

> ## There are lies, very bad lies and then there are statistics.

You can take almost anything and create a kind of statistic around it. Depending on what you compare it with you can make a certain statement based on that statistic.

If you present your claim in a powerful voice with conviction, most people will simply accept it as truth. So the combination of self-confidence with a certain claim can be a very powerful technique in sales.

You could say: *"90% of all Americans prefer to have coffee over tea in the afternoon."*

It is very difficult to prove this point otherwise. This statement might be completely false but if presented with the right tone and conviction, people will accept it.

> *Some sales people use statements that no one can prove and build their whole presentation around it.*

• **Another example:** *"Whoever doesn't buy this product is completely stupid."*
This statement implies that I think you are stupid if you don't buy the product and since you don't want to be known as stupid, you agree.

• **Another example:** *"According to a recent study three out of four men who make more than $100,000 per year drive a Mercedes."*
This statement is probably wrong. But in the right context, no one will question that statement.

• **Another example:** *"A study done by the mega Bank Credit Suisse reveals that there are 24.2 million millionaires in the world today. 41% of them live in the USA."*
This statement seems to be founded because the institute who issued this statement is very credible in the public eye. It has also details that no one can really prove otherwise. But is it really true? Who knows?

In general, you should not believe anything when you first hear it. You should always question things. Use common sense. For example, studies from Universities can be very misleading. So the University of Bordeaux in France will make you believe that their red win is actually beneficial for your health. Their studies will prove that. Another study will prove that alcohol in general will be damaging your health. So who do you believe? It is all in the eyes of the beholder and how and when a statement is presented.

Funnel question principle

This technique is very powerful because it will be built up with several questions. You start with a general question. After you ask an emotional question and make him aware of a problem or deficit. And finally you ask a provocative question so that the client will do or change something about his current situation.

Sometimes people are very stubborn and they think that everything is ok. But in order to make him aware that he needs to change something, you must sometimes break it into small and stupid steps or questions so that he will get it. Here is how it works:

Example 1:

- Can I assume that your retirement is absolutely secure and guaranteed? No.

- Are you getting $3000? Yes.

- $3000 per week? No.

- Do you like that?

Example 2:

- Am I right that your investments give you a return of 6% on average? Yes.

- Are you happy with it? More or less.

- Do you like giving away money?

Example 3:

- Do you pay taxes? Yes, of course.

- Do you like paying taxes? No.

- Would you like to get some of that money back?

> *1. General question*
> *2. Emotional question (show deficit)*
> *3. Provocative question*

The shocking technique

We also call this technique "The carp fish technique". The reason is because it is the same movement of a clients' mouth that the carp fish makes. The person is basically speechless and dumbfounded because he is in a short moment of shock. The client is not sure how to react to a certain question or statement.

Example:

- Mr. Client, I just told you all the advantages of this investment.
- Now all I have to do is to tell you the name of the bank that will secure your money.
- Well, here it is: two banks do the guarantee of your personal savings. One is from West Africa – United African Savings Bank, and the other one is a bank from Russia – Credit Social Bank. They are both really good at what they do. (Pause and silence)
- Do you even know these banks? No. (Pause and silence)
- Now honestly, do you like the fact that an African and Russian bank is safeguarding your hard earned money?
- No, not really. Everything sounded so good so far but I am really unsure about the banks.
- Well, in that case you can relax. I was just joking with you. Your money will be safeguarded by the biggest bank in Switzerland and in America: Citibank and UBS. (Laughing of client and huge sigh from relief)
- I would never offer you such a thing. But I just wanted to make a point how important it is to have the right partners. Please excuse my little joke. But you should have seen the expression on your face when I mentioned the African and Russian bank. (Both are laughing)
- Well, in that case I feel much better.

> *Why is this technique effective? There is a moment in your speech when you "shock" your client. For a couple of minutes, everything is up in the air and the client feels really unsure about everything.*

The idea is to shake up the client, shock him for a short moment and finally bring him back into a positive mood.

Most people are so relieved that they don't focus on anything else anymore. They get into a happy and positive mood because of your little joke, which will give you a perfect opportunity to go into the contract without any resistance from the client.

I have done this exact example over a hundred times and it worked each time. This whole thing seems a bit daring or provocative but it really works.

Jokes

Some of the best sales people that I have met were constantly telling jokes to their clients. They were so entertaining and funny that the entire mood was happy and positive and the product details never even mattered. The clients did the deal only because of the sales person.

Not everybody is able to play the funny guy all the time. But realize that nothing is more important than rapport and likeability when it comes to clients. The more your client likes you, the more likely will he do a deal with you. Period.

I am not saying that you should constantly be joking with your clients. But sometimes it helps to make a joke to change the mood or the direction of a presentation. Sometimes people can get bored with your sales presentation and they stop listening. They are only there because they feel obligated. But in that case you will never get a client to sign a deal with you.

> *A funny story or a joke at the right time*
> *can change everything and give you your desired result.*

If you are not great at telling jokes, don't worry. Use a funny statement once in a while until you get more comfortable and the more you use it, the better it will get.

Wait until you reveal your product to the last possible moment

This technique is being used to create and maintain curiosity. A lot of sales presentations are actually structured like this. You wait as long as you can until the last possible moment before you will reveal your product. By doing this, your client will give you his full attention through the entire presentation.

Example:

- *The product that I will show you is brand new. In Europe, it sold over a million times in the first week alone. You will not only look younger with this product but you will also feel much better. Studies have shown that you can actually save money with this product. There is a secret ingredient in the product, which I will tell you more about later. But before I get to the point, I want to let you know that you have been one of the lucky ones who have been selected to be here in this historic moment.*

- *I can imagine that you would like to know more about this wonderful product. So why don't we take a closer look at the development of the cosmetics industry.*

You will build up so many positive arguments during the presentation that it will be hard for the client to bring up any objections. Some of those presentations can go on for over an hour before the client actually knows what this is all about.

The human is the most curious animal in the world – it is not the cat!

So by keeping the attention high, you can talk about the advantages of your product without getting any kind of resistance. In the end, when you reveal your product, it will be the absolute high point of your presentation and people will love it.

Putting fear into your client

All humans have two basic motivations:

1. To gain pleasure   2. To avoid pain

If someone wants to lose weight he does it to look better and to get positive attention (to gain pleasure). But the stronger motivation for his to lose weight is to no longer be called fat or unattractive (to avoid pain). Maybe this person is so unhappy because he got rejected so many times and can't find a lover. Even though he wants to feel better he is much more motivated to avoid the pain of rejection and frustration.

> ## *Usually, the motivation to avoid pain is much greater than the motivation to gain pleasure.*

You can talk all day to a client and tell him how great your product will be for him and talk about all the positive advantages. But to really push the right buttons so that he will act, you will need to find a way to put a certain amount of fear into him so that he wants to avoid future pain.

Example: if you are selling life insurance you could go into detail about how his income will be reduced to 50% in case of an accident. How his family would potentially suffer. You could describe how he has to move from the good neighborhood into the bad neighborhood and how his children would be exposed to crime and drugs. You can tell him how he has to sell his car and from now on take the bus for 2 hours every day. And that he can no longer go to his favorite holiday spot.

All he has to do is to sign the contract and buy the life insurance for $50 per month to avoid all of these problems. You can tell him how he owes it to his family and that he would be irresponsible not to do it. This whole description will get his emotions cooking.

The more you can describe it and put negative images into it, the more effective it will be. The fear of losing everything needs to be so strong that he has almost no other option but to do the contract.

Fear is a negative emotion and it is very strong. A lot of people act out of fear. Even though I preach not to pay attention to fear in your own life, as a sales technique, it is extremely powerful.

Interrogation technique

In order to be able to influence your customer, you will have to know every important detail so that you can make sure you will lead him into the right direction.

Some people are very closed off and it is hard for a sales person to get through to them. But in order to succeed, you will need to know certain things; otherwise you will never close a sale.

The interrogation technique can be very aggressive in general and it forces your client to answer. You will ask a number of questions to get the information that you need.

In order to apply this technique, you can also do it in such a manner that you can still get the desired result but you ask nicely and with a smile. You will still ask the same direct questions but it will not come across as aggressive. You can even apologize for asking certain questions but ask them nevertheless. Example:

- And is it not true that you were at that location on the 25th of this month? (Continue without waiting for the answer)
- And is it not true also that you were seen with Mr. Smith there? (Continue without pausing)
- And how can you tell me otherwise if we have all the facts here on the table? (smile)

You can only use this technique once or twice during a conversation because it will come across as aggressive. And you must then make sure that you will change the mood back to a more positive mood.

Another kind of interrogation is based on the principle to simply ask everything – even very personal questions without hesitation. Sometimes coming across as being somewhat naïve people will not take it personally and forgive you for asking so bluntly. Example:

- Since when do you have this horrible sickness?
- How did it all start?
- What did the doctors say?
- How did you manage financially?
- Did you have to get a loan from the bank in order to survive?

You simply continue to ask until all the answers are on the table. Sometimes your client doesn't realize how much information he will actually give you.

> *Never be afraid to ask anything. Just do it. The more information you have about the client, the better you can use it to make a sale.*

Time pressure and making it rare

People will buy a product if you use three techniques:

1. Make it rare
2. Contrast principle
3. Time pressure

If a product is rare, it makes it much more valuable and desirable. People want things that are special and rare because it sets them apart from the crowd and makes them feel special.

> *If you have to act until a certain deadline or else you will lose the opportunity to get the product, you are more likely to buy it.*

In the infomercial you will hear a statement like this: "But you must act now within the next 15 minutes or else the offer will be gone." So they are using these techniques to make people buy the product.

But you must be aware that you have to use the time pressure technique with every client and every single time. Don't give him time to think about it. There is no "I have to think about it" allowed.

Just realize that the next day, your client will have forgotten 50% of what you just told him and in a week he will remember only 10%.

Therefore you must force him to make a decision now when he has all the facts.

> ## The more time he has to think about it,
> ## the less likely he is going to close the deal.

You need to let him know that he will lose the deal if he doesn't act now or within the next 24 hours. People hate losing an opportunity. Sometimes the fear alone of potentially losing the deal is what will get the client to act – not necessarily the product itself.

You can also say something like: I can give you 5% discount if you decide today. But tomorrow I can no longer offer you this discount.

> ## If something is available in abundance, it has no value.
> ## If everybody can have it, it is nothing special.

People like special things and they like status. Sometimes people are willing to pay much more for a product because it will set them apart from the crowd.

Take wristwatches for example. You can buy a Rolex for $25,000 or a watch with the same capabilities for $100. There are certain cars that are only produced with a limited amount of numbers. In order to buy a car like this you have to put astronomical prices.

> ## Make the product rare and use time pressure every single time.

Example:

- *Nowhere else in the world can you buy this product. You can only get it with me. You can't buy it on the Internet. This product is so special and we are the only organization that can sell it. But I cannot make any promises. People are crazy about it and it is possible that next week we will be completely sold out. So if you want to get it, you must give me an answer now. I might not be able to sell it to you anymore in a couple of days.*

Make yourself rare and position yourself as an expert

People like to deal with experts or specialists. The more important you appear to be, the more respect and credibility you will get from the client. If the client feels that you are simply just another regular sales person who is trying to make a sale, you will have a hard time to the clients' attention.

Sometimes we used a technique where a secretary would call up the client first and ask some general questions. Then she would say that she would try to place his file on the desk of Mr. Smith, the most respected expert in the firm. But she could not promise that he would call the client.

Then a few days later Mr. Smith calls up the client. He tells the client that he is not sure how that file landed on his desk and that normally he would only deal with multi-million dollar clients. But since he has the client on the phone now, he is willing to talk to him as an exception.

Mr. Smith, the sales person, has to position himself as an absolute expert and specialist who only deals with rich and important clients normally. He is making a huge exception this time and the client should be feel that it is a privilege to be able to deal with him.

The conversation and the level of respect that the client has toward the sales person is a lot different in that situation. If the client thought that he is dealing with average Joe, the whole sales process would go differently. You don't have to lie and pretend to be someone that you are not. But you need to value yourself and position yourself as an expert. You should be viewed and treated with the same level of respect that a doctor would get.

There was once an insurance sales agent in Switzerland who called up clients this way:
- *Hello Mr. Client, my name is Peter Miller. I am the most successful and best insurance agent in Northern Switzerland. You have probably already heard about me. I am giving you the opportunity to talk about your life insurance situation with me. I have only two appointments available this week: Thursday at 3 pm or Friday at 1 pm. After that I am booked out for the next two months. Which time suits you better?*

At first he appears to be totally arrogant but surprisingly it worked like a charm. He really was the most successful person in his industry and when he met with the client he wouldn't waste a lot of time, either. He would say: *"I have planned exactly 30 minutes for you. After that I need to leave. Let's get to the point. Do you prefer to be insured only a little bit or the right way? In that case I suggest you insure yourself with a sum of $500,000."*

Of course, there are also other ways to do this but if you give your client the feeling that you are an expert and that you are not needing him, you will get a lot more respect.

A lot of new sales people make the mistake that they are always available for the client and that they want all the time in the world. They have a submissive behavior and they let the client dictate the conversation.

Acting naïve

Even though you might know a lot more about your client and his situation, it is sometimes wise to act completely naïve and to pretend that you have no clue what is really going on.

The advantage of this technique is that to find out if your client is being completely honest with you or not. You will find out if he is lying to you and this way you have a much better basis for the conversation.

This technique is often used in negotiations. You don't tell the other person that you already know everything. You act as if you don't know all the facts. Sometimes this is good because you can find out if you were wrong about your assumptions and then change the strategy.

Always ask questions, even if you already know the answers.

Sometimes you are in for a surprise and it changes the course of the whole conversation.

Telling the client what he has to do

You would be surprised how some of my sales people have talked to CEOs of big companies. They yell at them and tell them what to do. They say things like: who do you think you are talking to? Do you have any idea who I am? Often the CEO was in his fifties and the sales person in his twenties. But sometimes the older generation is used to a harsher tone.

CEOs and leaders respect people who are strong. Those are also the people with money who can close bigger deals. They are usually the ones who talk down on their employees and no one dares to talk to them in a firmer manner. So if they encounter a person who is just as dominant as they are, they respect them more. Some people also need to be told what they should do. Especially clients who are hesitant need to be told to act. Example:

- Mr. Client, I simply cannot believe that you think this way! No stop acting like a little child and sign the contract because it is the best for you. You know it. If you continue to be so hesitant with other things in your life, it will never get better!

It really takes big balls to talk to a client like that. But depending on where they are from, it is working really well. We have dealt for example with a lot of German clients who are used to getting orders for their superiors. Sometimes it is the only way to get the respect and attention that you need. Often it is the last resort as a technique. Don't attack the client but it is ok to get loud sometimes and make a point. You would be surprised how powerful this can be.

Words can be very powerful

Words are simply definitions for specific pictures. Words have a lot more influence than we think. The way that you express things is very important and it can be done in several ways. I could basically say the same thing in three different ways but how they are being perceived is a lot different. Here is an example:

1. You might probably be mistaken.   2. You are wrong.   3. You are a liar.

All three statements are related to the same situation but it depends greatly which one you use. If I call someone a liar, I will provoke a lot of anger and negative emotions but if I use the first statement, things are neutral and no emotions are being brought on.

Certain words can trigger buying signals. Other words will hinder the sale. Therefore you must select your words very carefully and find out what sells and what doesn't sell.

The term "saving for the next 30 years" can be ok or neutral for one person but it can hinder the sale with another client. For someone 30 years is so long and far away that it will be a demotivation for him. Instead rather use the term "saving for the future" or "saving for unforeseen things that might occur later". This is much more soft and less dangerous.

Another difficult term can be "to pay". We associate paying with paying bills or with losing money. Instead of using "to pay" or "paying" you could use "transfer the money to your new account" or "set money aside". Sometimes it is only because of little words or expressions that make the difference whether you can make a sale or not. Therefore, analyze exactly what you say and see if you can replace potentially iffy expressions that might scare people.

> **People have three main channels how they receive emotions. Some are visual, some auditive and some are feeling-oriented (kinesthetic).**

Some people need to see a product, others need to feel it and others need to hear about it. If you can find out how your client ticks, you can use the right words that will trigger the best positive emotions in him.

- **Someone who is visual will use terms and wants to hear things like:**
I can see that you like this / As you can see... / This looks very good...

- **People who are more receptive to sound will prefer terms like:**
That sounds great / I can hear in your voice that there is still something that bothers you / My friend told me that this is the best model

- **And the feeling oriented person needs the following:**
I have a good feeling when it comes to this product / I feel that the time is right for you / This must make you feel like a million dollars

The more terms you use that are in line with your client the more success you will have to touch him on an emotional level.

Pre-sales techniques

The sales process begins when you first meet your client. Often, a sales person makes two appointments with a client. The first appointment is the gather all the information and to assess what the client needs and the second meeting is to present him with a solution or a product.

Most new sales people believe that the most important meeting is the second meeting because that is when you are trying to sell him a product. But in reality it is the first one because if you use the right pre-sales techniques and questions in the first meeting, you will have the deal already closed by 50%. There are a number of questions that you can ask your client in the first meeting and ask pre-closing questions. Let me give you some examples:

- I have just explained to you the basic characteristics of this product. What if I could present you with a similar solution the next time that we meet, would you be interested in looking at it?
- If you really liked the product proposal, would you take advantage of it?
- So do I understand it right that you would like me to go back to the office and try to find the best product that fits your needs?
- Ok, I will do that then and present you the solution next week.

If your client answers all these pre-closing questions in a positive way, you will basically already know that he is going to buy from you. By asking these questions, you don't put any pressure on him and he knows that he doesn't have to sign anything right now. So he is open and relaxed. But you start with asking some open questions and you ask in such a way that he agrees to consider your product the next time. This is already half the battle in selling.

> **The goal of pre-selling and pre-closing questions is to make the client aware of certain situations and solutions. You will use those techniques in the first meeting so that you know what to present in the second meeting.**

More pre-closing or pre-selling tools and questions:

- *Considering I could present you with an offer next time that would fulfill all these conditions and points that we just talked about, would you be willing to buy this product?*
- *If I could show you a solution that could solve this problem, would you take advantage of my proposal?*
- *What if I told you that we could resolve all these problems with only $200 per month? Would that be worth it?*
- *If I can show you how you can retire 5 years early. Would you consider hiring me?*

In case his response is not 100% clear or he brings up objections, you could say things like:

- *Of course. But if you really, really like what I will have to show you, would you at least consider it?*
- *Which conditions will have to be fulfilled for you to be 100% happy so that you would buy this product? Ok, then I will try to fulfill these points.*
- *So do I understand you correctly that if I present you with a solution next time that makes you 100% happy, would you then buy from me?*

Only if you get a positive answer or feedback in the first meeting by using pre-closing questions, you should move forward. If not, you will not close a deal and you will waste your time. You don't need a sure answer the first time. But you need a good indication that he is at least open to look at your proposal. If he responds positively, I also tell him that he should be excited to meet with me next time. I build up more curiosity and excitement and I will let him know that he will be very happy with the result.

Another way to use pre-selling techniques is to draw pictures while you are explaining things to your client. If he can see it on a piece of paper while you explain something, it is much more powerful and the next time you can use the same pictures and drawings to bring back what you have mentioned in the first meeting.

> *80% of closing happens in the first meeting.*
> *If you did a good job with your pre-closing questions, there is a good*
> *chance that you will close the deal in the second meeting.*

Dealing with price issues

> *Price is seldom a reason why clients don't buy a product.*

A study from Harvard University shows that 94% of all selling decisions are not based on price issues. Price is only important when it comes to commodities or raw products. The most important thing is to find out from your client why he is concerned about the price. Ask him if price is his only issue. It can be that price is simply an excuse.

Your job as a sales person is take away any possible objections about price in advance. You could say: I know that price is important but is it ok if we talk about it a little bit later on?

Focus on the needs of the client. The value of the product must appear to be much bigger than the price. Clients are more concerned with getting a fair price instead of getting a low price. If you focus on the advantages of the product, price is always relative and subjective.

If a client says that the product is too expensive then it is because the qualities of the products were not made clear to the client. The price is always in relation to the benefit. If the benefit seems to be less than the price, the client will feel that it is too expensive. But if he sees that all the advantages and benefits are greater than the price appears to be ok.

> *Don't defend the price and don't start a price discussion with a client. You*
> *can only lose. Make sure that the price is never the only factor but things*
> *like quality, service, time, benefits, etc. stand together with the price.*

Sometimes it is smart to start like this: Mr. Client, our product is the most expensive product compared to the competition. But let me tell you why this is the case. In the end you will find that it will be well worth it. So let me begin by explaining some of the features and advantages that the competition doesn't have.

By bringing up the price issue yourself, your client will not be able to use it against you later on as an objection. Often it is better to start with the price and not to shock the client with the price in the end of your sales presentation. If he is constantly thinking about the price and how much it will cost him, he will not listen properly or be open to the positive advantages of the product.

CHAPTER 5

BECOMING A
SUCCESSFUL
SALES PERSON

Success through selling

> *The activities and attributes that are responsible for becoming a successful sales person are more important than talent or knowing all the sales techniques.*

Selling is a mental game. Success only comes when your mental attitude is right. Top sales people think differently than average sales people. They ask different questions and their goal-setting attitude is the reason why they achieve higher sales results.

The law of cause and effect is a universal law of nature. It says that if you do what other successful sales people do, you will get the same results. So go and ask other successful sales people what they do exactly and then copy their strategies.

Top sales people always strive to be the best. Their ambition is so high that it is the main reason why they are on top of the monthly sales list.

If you also want to get to the top of the list, you must decide to get to the top. That decision seems obvious but if you really think about it, it comes with a lot of consequences. You will only get to the top if you really DECIDE to become the best in your field. Anything else is mere daydreaming.

Selling is a tool to achieve your personal goals. It is a mechanism for you to make money to get the things that you want in life.

Maybe you would like to buy a car or a house in the future. In order to achieve this goal, you will need money. Therefore, your motivation to buy a specific car, for example, will motivate you and drive you to work harder.

Selling more and earning more commissions will help you to buy your desired car faster. You can calculate how many sales meetings you have to set in order to achieve your goal.

> **"Life is either a daring adventure or nothing at all."**
> (Helen Keller)

No matter what you do in life. You always have to sell yourself or your ideas. Selling is the basis for every success. That is why it is so important to learn everything there is to learn about it.

The following 22 steps will give you the tools in regards of what you should DO to become a successful sales person.

Master the basic sales elements

In order to become a great sales person you must master the basic sales elements. Just like a tennis player must train the basic elements like volley, serve, forehand and backhand, you must become great in the basic elements. The basic elements are:

1. Communication skills, rhetoric and question techniques
2. Prospecting on the phone
3. Identifying needs and creating a deficit
4. Dealing with objections
5. Building rapport
6. Building trust
7. Analyzing the client's situation and finding a solution
8. Presenting
9. Closing
10. Service after the sale
11. Time Management
12. Pre-sales techniques and closing preparation
13. Mental attitude for sales people
14. Personal development and learning
15. Understanding the numbers game
16. Dress code
17. Professionalism and behavior
18. Making a first impression
19. Sales techniques
20. Creating a successful sales script

You must learn to become a master communicator if you want to be successful in sales. You can learn all the techniques to become a good sales person.

But in order to get new clients, the key is prospecting. Most sales people don't like prospecting because they get too much rejection. But the better you get in prospecting, the more you will like this activity. The sooner you make peace with prospecting, the faster you will move forward.

You should embrace it and make it your strength. Once you have decided to turn it into a strength everything will change for the better.

Every person either wants to gain pleasure or avoid pain. Often, you must first create a deficit in the client's situation so that he will see a need and want to change it accordingly. Being able to create a deficit means that you make the client aware of a problem or a potential problem. Once he is aware of it, he will have the motivation to do something about it. If you fail to create a deficit, people will never act because they believe that everything is okay with their situation.

When it comes to objections, you should also make peace with it – just like with prospecting. Basically, you will always get the same 5 to 10 objections. You should develop 2 to 3 standard answers and learn them by heart. Once you have done that there is nothing that can surprise you anymore.

Also, check your mental attitude when it comes to selling. Is there something that bothers you? Is there something that you are not convinced of yourself? You will only succeed if you have the right mental attitude when it comes to your professional as a sales person, your product and your company. You will fail miserably if your head is not straight. Seek the help of your coach if you need help.

Do you really understand the numbers game? Nothing should surprise you once you have really understood this principle. Nothing will seem impossible anymore.

In order to be a successful sales person you need to have the fire inside of you. This fire must burn and you should be excited. You will only be able to spark the excitement in your client if you are excited.

In order to become better in your field, you must become more competent. This means that you should learn all the facts about your products and your industry.

Decide to become the best in your field by learning everything there is to learn about it. The more technical knowledge you have, the more convincing you will be in a sales situation.

> **The main reason why people buy from you is because they like you and because they trust you. It is as simple as that.**

Do you really know the reasons how to develop trust? Is the way you dress absolutely perfect? Are you smiling and is your behavior confident? Are your communication skills precise and solid? Are you able to build rapport with your clients? Do you see yourself as a professional?

Building rapport is the basis for trust. If you are able to create a mood that is happy and where the client likes you, you have won half the battle. A client will only buy from you if he likes you.

> **You need to become an expert in developing emotional intelligence. By "feeling" how the other person feels, you can say the right things and lead the conversation in the right direction.**

Are you using praise and recognition when dealing with your clients? This is the biggest substitute for love. Most people crave praise and recognition.

You only have one chance to make a first impression. Therefore you must dress perfectly. Studies have shown that a dark blue suit with a conservative tie will convey most trust. A grey suit or a black suit is also acceptable. But you should always have a white or light blue shirt. Your tie can be a bit brighter and more colorful but should always be conservative.

And finally, are you able to consult different kinds of people? Do you know the main four personality types of people and are you able to deal with different people differently? Are you also able to deal with couples effectively? Look at the list and check the points that need improvement. Put together a learning and improvement plan for yourself.

Personal sales

Theory is important but only actual experience counts.

The good thing about selling is the ability to determine your income. The more appointments that you make the more money you will earn. The better the quality of your client segment the higher will be the average commission per client.

This is why you must know your personal sales numbers. Those numbers are percentages or quotas of each step in the sales process. But you can only get these numbers from your past activities. If you haven't made any sales activities yet, you can take general numbers from beginners in your field. The sales numbers relate to:

1. The number of contacts and addresses
2. The number of calls made
3. The numbers of appointments set
4. The number of appointment actually made

5. The number of second meetings
6. The closing rate
7. The average sale or commission per client
8. The monthly sales target

You have to start with your end goal. How much should be your monthly sales target? Let's assume that you would like to earn $10,000.

You must ask yourself how many contacts, names, lists, addresses or referrals you will need to accomplish this goal. Do you have enough and the right kind of contacts so that it makes sense to hit the phones?

How many sales calls do you need to make in order to get one appointment with a client? Let's assume that you will have to make 10 calls to get one appointment.

How many appointments will actually take place? How many are cancelled? How many are a waste of time? In general, 80% will be normal appointments and 20% will be canceled or moved.

So how many appointments will you actually need to have so that you can reach your target? How many more do you need to set? How often do you have to meet with a client in order to close a deal? How many people need to think about your offer? How many people will require a second or even a third meeting? How many deals can you close out of good 10 appointments? What is your closing rate? How much is your average commission per client?

Assuming that you can close 50% and your average commission is $500 per client, you will have the following numbers to work with:

- **Setting the right goals and planning the correct activities to reach your goal**
If you really know your numbers well, you can determine exactly what you must do in order to reach your sales target.

Average commission per client:	$500
Sales target:	$10,000
Clients closed:	20 clients
Closing rate:	50%
Actual sales appointments:	40 appointments
20% for cancellations	setting 50 appointments
10% calling rate	call up 500 people

If you earn $10,000 and divide it by 500 calls, then the result is $20 per call made. For every call that you make you will earn $20 – no matter what the outcome is. This will make it psychologically easier to deal with rejection.

Once you have done this a few times and keep track of all your numbers you can determine where potential problems lie so that you can improve your overall sales result. You can focus each month on improving one area and they to improve the percentage in that step of the process.

> **There is nothing that you cannot accomplish if you know your numbers and try to improve your skills in each step.**

Sales is like math – everything is a numbers game

> *Everything is a numbers game.*
> *The more people you can contact the higher will be your sales result.*

When it comes to financial success in sales you need to realize that everything is a numbers game. There is really only one rule: The more people you talk to, the more prospects you will get and this will improve the probability to make a sale.

Everything is based on the law of cause and effect. The more causes that you set by calling more people, making more appointments, the more deals can you close. The busy and active sales people will always outperform the lazy ones.

If you want to earn a certain amount of money in a year, you must break it down to a monthly average amount. If you want to earn $300,000 per year, you must earn $25,000 per month on average. If you can sell on 25 days of the month, you must make at least $1000 in commission per day. If you can make $500 in commissions per closed deal, you have to close two deals per day on average. This is your basic goal setting calculation of what you want to achieve.

But now you must know your actual numbers from your activities. What are you numbers or quotas in each area? If your closing rate is 50%, then you must have 4 sales opportunities with clients each day. If you know that 20% will move, change or cancel the appointment, then you must set 5 new appointments each day.

Depending on the quality of your contacts and by having the perfect target group, your numbers might increase dramatically.

> *Basically, success in sales is predictable. It is like math.*
> *You can calculate it. All you need is self-discipline*
> *to ensure that you do the right activities.*

In order to change or improve something you must analyze your numbers and figure out what could be done to improve each area. Ask yourself the following questions to improve your results:

- Where could you get better names or contacts?
- How could you improve your prospecting success?
- Is there a way to get referrals or to get clients to be better prepared for you?
- How can you ensure that people will actually show up to the appointment and not cancel or move it?
- How can you make sure that you can close a deal in the first appointment?
- How can you improve your closing rate?
- How can you increase the average sales commission per client?

> *"Successful people ask better questions,*
> *and as a result, they get better answers."*
> (Tony Robbins)

Defining your target market and your ideal client

> *Finding new clients is the most important thing in sales.*
> *Without new clients there is no future.*

Your income and all your goals are dependent on getting new clients. That is why you should really become an expert in this topic.

A lot of people have the wrong strategy when it comes to finding new clients. Some people believe that the whole world is their potential customer. If they are out of contacts, they take the phone book and start calling from the letter A or they talk to strangers on the street and believe that they could have a lucky punch.

This is a very unprofessional strategy and is based on luck. It is very inefficient and disheartening because an inexperienced new sales person will get so much negative rejection that he will fail for sure.

> **Doing cold calling is one of the worst strategies and is no longer effective in today's day and age.**

Even if you are willing to succeed no matter what the cost, you will burn out fast.

> **You need a real strategy and not just a shotgun approach and hope that someone will close by chance.**

Your potential group of clients is only theoretically unlimited. You cannot expect that everyone will buy your products or services. You will need a specific target market otherwise you will waste too much energy and the result will not be satisfying.

Ask yourself the following questions:

- Who is your ideal client?
- What kind of age group or range does he belong to?
- Is he male of female?
- What kind of work does he do?
- What is the income range?
- What are typical characteristics?
- What kind of hobbies do your clients most likely have in common?
- What kind of places or locations do these people do to on a regular basis?
- What kind of club, groups or organizations do they belong to?
- What kind of magazines do they read?

The better you can answer these questions, the better clearer you can identify your target market. Once you have done that you need to solely focus on this group and no one else. You will be much more successful if you focus on the right group.

Now ask yourself where you can find these people:

- Are there lists from list brokers that you can buy?
- Can you get a membership in the same organization like some of these people?
- Where should you advertise so that only your ideal client will read it?
- How can you get the first list of potential clients together and then work on a referral basis after that?

Example: let's say that you sell horse saddles. If you put an ad in a big general magazine or newspaper your response or output will be very low. But if you advertised in a horse magazine the people who read it are more likely to be in your target group and therefore the result or output would be much higher.

Finding new clients and getting started

There are four strategies that you can use to get started in any sales job.

- ### *Strategy 1: Personal contacts*
Some of the immediate results and successes can come from people that you already know. Everyone knows about 200 to 300 people in their personal circle.

You should brainstorm for a few hours and write down every last name that you have ever encountered in your life. You should go through your entire history or schools, jobs, clubs, relatives, associations, military, church, etc. and write down the people that you have ever met.

The main key is that you don't judge or cross out anybody from your initial list. Just get it on paper. You will be surprised how many people you will remember. Once you have finished the list you can ask yourself the following two questions:

1. Who on my list is a potential client?
2. Who on my list is NOT a potential client but can give me referrals for other clients?

> ### *The main advantage with people that you already know or have a connection to is the trust factor.*

If you can get a referral from someone then 50% of the trust level is already established and it will be much easier for you to close a deal.

• Strategy 2: Referrals of existing clients or contacts

The most efficient way to get new clients is to get referrals. Because of an existing relationship you will have it much easier to get the appointment because the new potential clients already trusts your existing client. He would not have given out his contact details if it really weren't a good thing that you are offering. It doesn't even matter too much whether he has been informed in advance or not.

Sometimes your client can talk too much and destroy your chances with a new potential client because the curiosity will be gone. The least that you can expect is that the new potential client will listen to what you have to say due to the relationship with the person who gave you the referral.

I have worked six years as a financial planner and I solely worked with referrals. I never had to do a cold call. I am persistent with each existing client and asked without exception for a list of at least 10 to 20 referrals. Once you are in a circle of good clients your life as a sales person can become really easy.

• Strategy 3: Networking

Another strategy is to go to networking meetings. The more people you meet, the more opportunities will open up to you. However, I must warn you that a lot of people who are going to networking meetings are looking for new clients themselves.

Most of them are broke and are looking for new clients to make money. You will not really find rich people there. But depending on your product or service it might not matter too much. You could also consider some of them as people who can refer you to other people.

- ***Strategy 4: Marketing activities to support your sales calls***

A better way than doing cold calling from the phone book is to support your phone activities with a marketing activity. Studies have shown that you will increase your calling rate by 1000% if you send a personal letter to your prospects a few days in advance in the mail. Since this is a cold contact, you can make a reference to the letter that you have sent and it will be your opening.

Another opportunity is to run an ad and offer something for free. Or instead of cold calling you can have a free downloadable brochure or piece of information where you can follow up.

But it is always better to have something than nothing when it comes to cold calling. Sometimes you can just get a list from a club or association and simply start your conversation by talking about the club.

Sometimes, there is only one thing to do: you must talk to as many people as possible in order to find a new solution or strategy.

Segmentation

A-clients know other A-clients.
B-clients know other B-clients.
C-clients know other C-clients and D-clients.

In general, you must differentiate between A, B and C clients. A-clients have the biggest potential, B-clients are average and C-clients are below average.

The more A and B clients you have the more sales you generate. The more you deal with people from this segment, the more referrals and other clients will also come from the same segment. Once you realize this fact, the faster you will change your focus.

You could also do your own segmentation of your clients. This could be based on income:

A-clients = Income over $100,000 per year
B-clients = Income between $50,000 and $100,000 per year
C-clients = Income below $50,000 per year

Some people give up their sales job because they spend too much time in the C-segment. It is hard to fight for every little commission and you get a lot of *"sorry, I can't afford your product"* objections.

Maybe the only thing you need to change your motivation is to change your client segment. Realistically, you can't only have A-clients. It will always be a mix. Most new sales people start with the C-clients because they need to make their experiences first.

> *You should realize that it takes exactly the same amount of time and effort to deal with an A-client than with a C-client.*

Some sales people are very particular about this. They refuse to deal with anybody who is not an A-client. And if you are consistent with this approach, you will do much better.

If you see yourself as an expert who solely deals with the best people, your whole approach changes from being an annoying high-pressure sales person to a professional consultant and expert.

The 80/20-rule

> *80% of your success comes from your attitude – 20% from your skills.*

The 80/20-rule is one of the main rules for success in sales. It says that 20% of the time you invest into certain activities will bring you 80% of the result. It also says that 20% or your clients will bring you 80% of your total sales result.

Successful sales people have found out how they must use their time and energy to get at least 80% of their result.

The 80/20-rule is applicable in almost every area of selling. You can use it to analyze your clients and their potential, your own sales activities and your earning ability.

Ask yourself which 20% of your time and energy will yield 80% of the result. Which activities do you need to do more of so that you can excel in your overall sales result?

If you realize that prospecting will give you 80% of your results, then you should do more prospecting. If you realize that A-clients will give you 80% of your results, then you should focus on more A-clients.

Self-confidence and fear

> *Fear is the main reason for failure. If you really think about it and decide that you will no longer be afraid of anybody or anything, there is no limit to what you can achieve.*

Fear paralyzes people. It makes people hesitant and scared. Top sales people confront their own fears and then decide to move forward despite them. If you the same, your life will change. The more self-confidence you have, the more successful you will be. The three main fears that hold you back are:

1. Fear of failure   2. Fear of rejection   3. Fear of success

If you have fear of failure you will delay things unnecessarily and you will avoid situations that could lead you to the next level. If you are afraid of rejection you will not whole-heartedly make phone calls and avoid calling times as much as possible. You will find excuses why you must do other things instead. Once you have overcome those two first fears there is really nothing that can hold you back.

Interestingly, some people have fear of success. They start to have a little bit of success and then they sabotage themselves. They subconsciously connect success with pain. Here are some things that can help you to overcome your fears and build more self-confidence:

1. Act already today as if you were successful. Don't think too much about it. Just do it. If your subconscious mind believes that you are already successful, you will create the outer circumstances to make it a reality.
2. Set small, daily goals that you can achieve. For example: Today I am going to call 10 people. This is absolutely doable and realistic. But this will add to your self-confidence.
3. No more excuses! Take charge of your own life – no matter what the circumstances are.
4. Use your own time well. Only focus on income-generating activities.
5. Read one book per week. Continue to learn about sales and marketing.
6. Decide never to give up – no matter what! This is the strongest factor of them all. Once you have really decided never to quit, there will be no plan B. You will stop doubting your career and have more emotional energy because you give yourself no other choice.

How many clients do you really need?

You don't need the whole world to make money. In most industries it is enough if you a client base of 200 to 300 clients. With this amount of clients you will be able to get repeat business to sustain the same annual income that would normally make.

This way you will focus more on servicing the existing clients and you don't have to get new clients as much anymore. If you like your industry you should make a plan to build up about 300 clients.

If you start out new you should begin with a list of at least 1000 very good potential clients. First, you should start to gather all the names and lists that fit your target market.

In order to make sales you have three choices:
1. You make a new sale
2. Your existing client makes a repeat purchase
3. You increase the average amount per sale

If you want to make $100,000 per year and you need 100 clients for this goal then the average commission is $1000 per client. If you can motivate half of your existing clients to buy again in the same year then your income is $150,000 or 50% more. If you are able to increase the average amount from $1000 to $2000 per client then you will have doubled your income.

As you can see, you have three options to increase your overall sales target with the same amount of people.

Time management and weekly planning

> *What would I miss in my life if I never felt financially secure?*
> *What kind of effect would it have on my relationships, health,*
> *stress level, self-confidence and my desire for freedom?*
> *How would I feel if I still had to work so very hard late in life?*

You can change everything with time management. Time management is a tool to complete more tasks and achieve more goals in a shorter period of time.

> *If you use time management effectively, you can save years of hard work.*

Here are some basic tips for sales people:

1. Plan your prospecting time as a set time in your weekly calendar

You should block off at least 5 hours per week for prospecting activities. These 5 hours are just as important if not more important than an actual meeting with a client. I used to choose one evening per week and Saturdays from 11 am to 1 pm. These times were fix in my calendar and I would never move or change them because I needed to ensure that I would always have enough new appointments going forward.

2. If you work, you should work all the time

People go to the office and waste time talking or socializing with others. They take long coffee or cigarettes breaks and take extended lunches. They waste a few hours every day while they are at the office. At the end of the day they didn't really accomplish much but they feel like they worked all day because they were spending all these hours at the office.

It is better to work 5 hours with full power and then take half of the day off. Make it a habit to work all the time when you are at work. But when you have your leisure time, don't work.

3. Plan meetings close together

Instead of having a meeting at 10 am, one at 2 pm and then one at 6 pm, you should try to keep your meetings close together. This will give you more flexibility and freedom.

4. Don't drive around all over the place

Time is money. If you have one meeting in LA and the next in San Diego, then you waste valuable driving time by driving around too much. You should plan your meetings when you are in a certain area anyway and try to keep the locations close together.

5. Make your meetings at the office if possible

The less time you lose by driving around the more productive you can be. People are happy to come to you if they believe that you are a specialist in your field. You can also make the first initial meeting at the client's place and then the second follow up meeting at your office.

6. Set at least three meetings per day with clients
In order to be successful you must have enough opportunities to make a sale. Setting at least three client meetings per day is a minimum. If you don't do that you are either lazy or don't plan well.

7. Already know in advance when and how many meetings you will have in a week
You should have empty boxes in your weekly calendar where you want to set a client meeting. It is like playing the submarine board game. You need to fill in the empty spots.

	Sunday	Monday	Tuesday	Wednesday	Thursday	Friday	Saturday
7am		GYM	GYM	GYM	GYM	GYM	
8am	FAMILY TIME						
9am		A	M		A		
10am							A
11am			M				
12am							P
1pm		M	M	M	M	M	
2pm							
3pm		M	P	M	M	M	
4pm							
5pm		M	P	M	M	M	
6pm							

M = Meetings   *P* = Prospecting   *A* = Administration

8. Plan about 70% of all appointments fixed in advance
In order to plan successfully for the future and to reach your goals you must have a minimum amount of client meetings. It is better to have a plan that is about 70% planned and structured in advance than not to have any fixed plan at all.

> *If you think you should simply see what happens,*
> *you will not be productive and not reach your goals.*

You shouldn't plan out 100% in advance, either. Things always change and need to be somewhat flexible.

> **Success planning = income planning = weekly planning**

Become a great communicator

> **Every successful person is automatically a great sales person and communicator.**

If you have understood this principle once and for all, you will always be successful in life – no matter what you do. Selling is a skill that can be learned.

There are a lot of great books and courses that can teach you how to become a better sales person and communicator. My favorite books in are (they were mandatory in my first sales organization):

- *"How to win friends and influence people"* (Dale Carnegie)
- *"How I raised myself from failure to success in selling"* (Frank Bettger)
- *"Think and grow rich"* (Napoleon Hill)

If you do nothing else but read those three books, you will get enough knowledge and inspiration to become a better sales person. I can promise you that. The thing with advice is that you need to take it.

I have over 20 years of sales experience and I was the best in my organization as a sales team leader. In order to succeed you will have to keep learning and improving and reading books is a part of that.

There is nothing better than actual real life sales experience. But you don't have to make every single mistake that most beginners make.

It is very easy to fail in sales. In fact, you will fail all the time and it takes a strong mental attitude to stay positive and focused. But if you keep at it and pay that price, the reward will be great.

> *The basis of being a great sales person is to improve your communication skills. This is something that will help you in every aspect of your life — not just at work.*

Communication and persuasion skills mean power.

You can get almost anything that you want in life if you know how to ask for it. If you become a great negotiator, you will be better off in anything that you do.

Extroverted or introverted personality?

> *You must be born as a sales person. That is a fact.*
> *First, you must be born and then you can become a sales person.*
> *So basically everybody can become a sales person.*

We have this myth that extroverts are better salespeople. As a result, extroverts are more likely to enter sales; extroverts are more likely to get promoted in sales jobs. But if you look at the correlation between extroversion and actual sales performance - that is, how many times the cash register actually rings - the correlation's almost zero.

Success in sales is dependent on how many deals you can close.

Because extroverted sales people are often perceived as too aggressive or slimy, a lot of the busy and active but apparently introverted sales people come across more as a consultant and because of that they create more trust with the client.

I have seen many "introverted" sales people who had far better sales results than the "big talkers". They were focusing on making many appointments and because of the numbers game, their results were always much better. In my opinion it doesn't matter how much talent you have or how well you can draw attention to yourself.

> *When it comes to sales,*
> *the ones who are most self-disciplined always win the game.*

When it comes to your personality, you must be driven and you must want to deal with clients. If someone is introverted and numbers-oriented he might be happier as an accountant or financial analyst. However, a person who seems to have these traits but wants to succeed in a sales profession can learn the techniques to better deal with clients and become successful.

The problem with many extroverted people is that they have the talent for communication and sales but a lot of them are lazy or have the wrong attitude when it comes to working in sales. They are so good that they only do minimal work and therefore the results are often also minimal. If they actually put in the effort, they would be great. But the key here is to understand that talent alone will not make you a successful sales person.

> *Success as a sales person comes from*
> *using your talent and skills, improving them and then*
> *making enough sales contacts to ensure sales success.*

As long as your personality is driven, self-disciplined and active, it doesn't really matter whether you have a tendency to be rather introverted or extroverted.

Analyze the critical success factors from 1 to 10

In sales, the difference between success and failure often lies in small details. You should go through all the critical success factors and judge yourself in each area from 1 to 10. The areas are:

1. Prospecting

2. Segmentation

3. Problem identification

4. Presentation

5. Dealing with objections

6. Closing

7. Time Management

Give yourself a grade from 1 to 10 in each of those areas and then look at the result. Where is your weakest factor? Where is your second weakest factor? Once you realize that you have potential for improvement in one or two areas, then go to work and improve them right now. Everything that has a value of 7 or less needs immediate attention and training.

> ***You are only as strong as your weakest link***
> ***in the critical success factors.***

You can also create a second list that is more extensive or detailed. It is all based on your type of sales position. Here is another example:

1. Sales know-how in general

2. Service

3. Getting referrals

4. Product knowledge

5. Giving group presentations / presentation skills

6. Number of clients / contacts

7. Another factor

Of course, the list will look different based on where you work and what types of products that you sell. But the main goal is to make an analysis of your own strengths and weaknesses in the most important areas that are responsible for success.

This exercise should give you more clarity so that you can improve your weakest areas and therefore improve the overall result.

Incremental improvements

In order to get better, you can't all of a sudden improve 100% in each area. That is not humanly possible. But you can improve each area by 10%. You can make certain things a little bit better and improve them by 10%.

You should look at sales like a human organism. If you have a problem with high-blood pressure for example, you should change your lifestyle. In this case you would eat healthier, exercise more and cut out salt and sugars. After a few weeks, your high-blood pressure problem will improve.

But interestingly, these changes would not only affect your high-blood pressure and make positive changes in that one area. It would also have a positive effect in all other areas. It would improve you cholesterol, your lungs, your heart, your digestion, etc. So changing and improving one thing will have a positive effect on the entire system. The same is true for selling.

> *Once you improve one area, it will have a positive effect on all the other areas as well and on the outcome of the entire result.*

If you did more prospecting and you learned new techniques and how to handle objections better, do you think it would have an effect on the entire sales result? Of course it would! Mathematically here is the proof:

Area 1 (Prospecting): $1.00 \times 1.1 = 1.10$
Area 2 (Segmentation): $1.10 \times 1.1 = 1.21$
Area 3 (Problem identification): $1.21 \times 1.1 = 1.33$
Area 4 (Presentation): $1.33 \times 1.1 = 1.46$
Area 5 (Objections): $1.46 \times 1.1 = 1.61$
Area 6 (Closing): $1.61 \times 1.1 = 1.77$
Area 7 (Time Management): $1.77 \times 1.1 = 1.94$

You start with a value of 1.0 in the one area like prospecting. You are today a level 1.0 with your current skills. If you improve your current condition by 10% you will become a 1.1 in that area. Then go improve the second area by 10% and so on. In the end you will have an overall improvement of 94%!

> ***You can almost double your sales***
> ***by improving each of the seven key areas by 10%.***

By improving one area you will improve all the other areas as well.

Referrals are the foundation for success

No one really likes cold calling or prospecting. It is hard work and you get a lot of rejection. Often, good sales people start to doubt themselves or their company if a bad steak goes on for too long. This creates stress and negative emotions.

There are much better ways to operate than doing cold calling. Think about it: If you had a great service experience when you got your car fixed and got 25% off the regular price would you not recommend that service company to a friend? Would you not tell your family and friends about it and suggest that they should also go there? Of course you would!

In all kinds of regular activities in life, we constantly make recommendations for places to go to or businesses where we got a good deal. This is a normal part of life. For you as a sales person it is much easier to get a new appointment if another person referred you. If you had a client who was really happy with your service and he told someone else about it and then you contacted that person, don't you think that it would make your prospecting activities so much easier? Your client would never recommend or refer you if you did a bad job, right? So because his friend already trusts him and his opinion, he will at least check out what you have to say or to offer, right? If not, he would have never given you that name.

> *Working with referrals will make your life as a sales person 10 times easier and more effective. The only thing that you must do is to be consequent about asking for referrals!*

Asking for referrals should be part of your sales strategy. It should be an integral part of the whole process. Here is how you can do it:

You need to make an agreement with your new client in advance before you offer him advantages. You basically make a deal with him.

You tell him that you will give him all kinds of advantages and rebates for free but in return you expect him to give you referrals in the end. Once you make that agreement with your new client and he receives great service from you, he will gladly give you a number of people that you can contact later on.

But sometimes an agreement alone is not enough. You must make sure that you have developed great rapport and trust. You must be professional in the way your look and act so that the client will not have to worry about your service. And you must be consequent in your expectations otherwise you will not give away your tips and services for free.

I typically expect at least 10 names from my clients. I prepare an empty list where they can put in the names of their friends that they will refer to me.

Once I meet with the client I make the following agreement: In my first meeting with him I will make a needs analysis and figure out what he needs and wants. In my second meeting I will present my solutions. Instead of him paying me I expect him to give me the list with the contacts if he was happy with my consultation in the end.

I have done this in over 3000 client meetings without exception. I have always received referrals from my clients because I asked and I was consequent in my approach. The ones who refused never became my clients anyway.

Telemarketing: 5 calls per day – 1250 calls per year more

> *Sometimes simply doing one little thing on a consistent basis can change the overall outcome.*

Most sales people don't like prospecting or telemarketing. The effort and rejection is the main reason why people don't do it in the first place.

But let's assume that you are in a position where you can get leads from a different kind of source or through a marketing activity that your company has set up. So in your case you don't really have to do any kind of cold calling or telemarketing.

Now just imagine for a moment that you can make peace with telemarketing. You don't have to switch entirely to telemarketing. But here is one question for you:

If you simply made 5 additional calls per day during 250 working days per year and therefore made 1250 calls more, do you think it would have a positive effect on your yearly result?

Of course it would! No matter how good or bad you are at prospecting, you would certainly have a few more clients out of the 1250. You would make more money and because you did so many calls, you would also automatically get better at it over time.

Always be honest with yourself and with your clients

> *"Honesty and integrity are absolutely essential for success in life - all areas of life. The really good news is that anyone can develop both honesty and integrity."*
>
> (Zig Ziglar)

Honesty and integrity should be your main values. Always be honest with your clients but also with yourself. Look at your weekly schedule and ask yourself honestly if you really did everything that you could do to fully reach your potential. Never be lazy or scared to work too hard.

Also, make sure you keep your clients' interests at heart. Try to put yourself in your client's shoes and see the situation from his point of view. Figure out what he wants and what motivates him. Honesty is the number one reason that clients expect from you.

Honesty is closely related to being realistic. You need to have a realistic view of your activities and your personal situation in order to change it for the better.

Most sales people are dreamers and spend time hoping that the future will get better. But this is not how success works. You need to be 100% honest with yourself and analyze your activities and level of skills so that you can improve them.

Be a professional in everything that you do

Top sales people are professional in everything that they do. Always take care of small details and communicate well with your clients. See yourself as a problem solver rather than a high-pressure sales person. Never be lazy when it comes to clients. Small details can change everything. They can determine whether you will make a sale or get referred. If you build a reputation of being absolutely professional, you will get further than you can even imagine today.

See yourself as an expert and consultant rather than a sales person. Position yourself as a specialist like a doctor and demand the same kind of respect from your clients.

> *If you act like a professional, you will get a more committed reaction from your clients back.*

Think about it this way: If you were to have brain surgery would you as a patient prefer to have it performed by a general practitioner or by the brain specialist who performs two surgeries per day?

Keep informed and keep learning

> *We must accept the fact that learning*
> *is a lifelong process and it never stops.*

Most of what we know about sales comes from a world of information asymmetry, where for a very long time sellers had more information than buyers. That meant sellers could hoodwink buyers, especially if buyers did not have a lot of choices or a way to talk back.

But things have changed with the Internet. People can get all the information that they need themselves. They can verify everything and compare companies and prices. Because of this, your job has slightly changed.

You must find the areas where your clients need you and where you can add value. You must offer them knowledge that they can't easily get on the Internet.

Therefore you must become more competent about your industry and your products. You must become a specialist in your field and always know more than your clients. You must stay informed and continue to read, learn and go to seminars.

> *"A man only learns in two ways, one by reading,*
> *and the other by association with smarter people."*
> (Will Rogers)

Self-motivation, desire and determination

> *Nothing can stop a man with the right attitude.*
> *Nothing can help a man with the wrong attitude.*

Desire is the key to motivation, but it's determination and commitment to an unrelenting pursuit of your goal basically a commitment to excellence that will enable you to attain the success you strive for.

The secret of success is learning how to use pain and pleasure instead of having pain and pleasure use you. If you do that, you're in control of your life. If you don't, life controls you. You should realize that success is always in your head. It is a mental game. That is the real secret to success.

Part of learning and moving forward is to make mistakes. You don't learn to walk by following rules. You learn by doing, and by falling over. The main thing is that you keep getting up and continue to move forward despite your failures. If you never give up, you cannot fail.

In order to develop an unshakable desire to succeed, you must first ask yourself what you really want to achieve in life. You must set goals and then hang them on a wall where you can see them every single day. You can cut out pictures and put them into a dream book. You should visualize daily and dream for at least five minutes.

Goal setting – plan for the whole year in advance

Setting goals is the first step in turning the invisible into the visible. In order to know what you should be doing every day, you need to set goals. You need to take your yearly sales and commission goal and then break it down on a monthly basis. Then you need to make a plan to decide exactly what activities you need to do. So basically, you need to plan your activities based on your numbers and not just set a sales target that is nice to have.

You need to make a plan, set a deadline and quantify your goals. You should have long-term goals and short-term goals. In sales a long-term goal is two to three years, a medium term goal is 12 months and a short-term goal is a month. You need a specific plan and mini goals. Only the mini-goals and daily activities will help you to move forward.

You should set a goal for the entire year in advance. Ask yourself what you really want to have, do and be? Based on your dreams, you must then set a goal.

Remember: selling is a tool to help you to get the things you want. But goal setting must be done right or else it won't work. Example:

A dream or a wish is: I would like to have a Ferrari.
A goal is: I would like to have the Ferrari Testarossa model F110 by December 31st 2015 for the price of $250,000.

In order to reach your goal you must take the $250,000 and break it into activities.

Remember, you can calculate how long it will take you to buy this car if you know your numbers.

You alone are responsible for your results

> *"Sales are contingent upon the attitude of the salesman,*
> *not the attitude of the prospect."*
> (W. Clement Stone)

And finally, be aware that you are always responsible for everything that happens to you. If you fail to have a good sales result at the end of the month, you must realize that there is no one but you to blame. It is never someone else's fault; it is always your fault.

The reasons why you fail to achieve a sales target are never the client, the market or your boss. You are always responsible for your targets and no one else.

> **"The meeting of preparation with opportunity generates the offspring we call luck."**
> (Tony Robbins)

There is no such thing as luck. Luck comes from creating a lot of opportunities that you have initiated. By the law of averages, you will end up with a bigger client once in a while because you have done the necessary causes. You can call it luck but luck is the result of preparation and action. It is based on cause and effect.

The amount of good luck coming your way depends on your willingness to act. Luck and hard work always go together hand in hand.

CHAPTER 6

CREATING & GIVING
AMAZING
PRESENTATIONS

Albert Mehrabian – making an impression

Albert Mehrabian has found out that 55% of a presentation is visual, 38% is the voice and that only 7% is the content or the words!!!

> **So if 93% is non-verbal, then a lot of non-verbal factors play an important role.**

Things like body language, your facial expressions, your gestures, your voice or the way you emphasize things have a huge impact on your overall presentation.

Hitler's speeches are very simple and the content is ridiculous but the way he presented and the way the spoke with his intensity influenced a whole nation.

The mental attitude about your topic is also very important. What do you really think about the topic that you are presenting? Are you convinced about the content yourself? Are there any objections that you might fear from the audience? Little signals that point to your insecurities or words like "basically" or "aehm" will diminish the power of your message.

> **That is why you should always be very well prepared and know exactly what you are going to say.**

It is not about giving as much information as possible but to present one main message even if your presentation will be shorter.

In 1941 Winston Churchill was once asked to give a speech in front of hundreds of people. Everybody was waiting in great anticipation for this speech. He went up on stage and waited for a while until everybody was quiet. Then he paused for a long time. Finally he began to speak and said: *"Never give up, never give up, never give up!"*.

That was the end of his speech. But until this day people will still remember this speech. The main thing is not to blabber as much as possible but to give the audience one important message. And that is what you should be doing as well.

Structure of a presentation

In regards to structuring a presentation, it is advisable to know in advance what your main message will be. The following tool I have learned from Manoj, a famous sales trainer from Hong Kong. I have tested and tried it several times and it works just great because it is so simple.

Imagine that your presentation is like a house with three columns. There is a roof, three columns that are founded or anchored into three cement buckets.

• The roof is the main message or statement that you want to get across.
• The three columns are your three main arguments that support your main message.
• The buckets of cement stand for the facts, detailed information, examples or proof to give your arguments additional support.
• And finally, you have the conclusion as the foundation of your house at the very bottom.

Every time you have to hold a quick speech, even if it is only for 5 minutes, it helps to be clear about the structure of your presentation.

1. What is the main message?
2. What are the main three arguments that support that message?
3. What are the facts to each argument that give it additional support?
4. What is the conclusion?

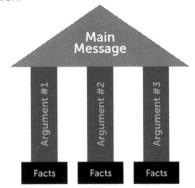

I have done several little tests and presentations with my sales people. I gave them a topic and a little bit of preparation time and the goal was to make a 5-minute presentation. Then we filmed the first presentation. Afterwards I explained to them the model with the three columns and then they had to prepare another presentation with the same topic based on that model. They had to first define the structure with the respective statements or arguments. We also filmed the second presentation and in the end we compared both of them.

The difference was absolutely incredible. The quality of the second presentation was so much better and even though most of those sales people were beginners, they appeared to be experienced sales people.

Let me give you an example: let's say you had to give a presentation on the topic of investing into gold stocks. Then it would look as follows:

- **Opening statement (claim or general statement)**
"Gold stocks are the best alternative to blue chips stocks and have the biggest growth potential."

Argument 1: Average performance of gold stocks compared to other stocks
Argument 2: Growth potential
Argument 3: Gold price development

- **Facts to argument 1:**
In the last 80 years stocks have had an annual performance of 8% and have outperformed all other asset classes. In the last 5 years the SP500 (Index of the 500 biggest companies in the US) have risen 20% on average during this time frame. Gold stocks have had a performance of 100% during the same time frame. Even though gold stocks are more volatile, the have performed much better than the overall stock market.

- **Facts to argument 2:**
The annual demand for gold is 3800 tons. But only 2500 tons of gold are produced. Because of this deficit the demand for gold will go up. New markets like China and India will need more gold and the central banks will have to stock up on their gold reserves. They used to hold 4% and today they only have 1%.

- **Facts to argument 3:**

The gold price has developed from $250 per ounce to over $2000 per ounce in the last 15 years with current prices around $1500. Most experts predict that gold will go past $3000 per ounce in the next 5 years due to fundamental economic factors.

- **Conclusion:**

Blue chip stocks have only developed slowly and they current have a limited growth potential. A lot of arguments support that an investment into gold stocks will be a much better investment choice.

Opening your presentation

> **Top speakers start their presentation with a strong opening to capture the attention of the audience.**

They never start their talk before there is absolute silence in the room and everybody is paying attention. If they don't do that, they lose their authority. In the very beginning the audience should understand what they would gain from listening to the presentation. The question *"what is in it for me?"* needs to be answered.

The main goal at the start of each presentation is to get the full attention of your listeners. You will achieve this best if you have a strong opening. There are a number of impressive ways to do that. You can surprise your audience, shock them or present interesting facts.

Here are a number of ideas on how to open your speech or presentation:

- **Anecdotes or stories**

You can make a joke or tell them an anecdote. Anecdotes have a lower risk than jokes. Chose a story that suits well to your given topic.

- **Shock opening**

Example: *"Every 60 seconds a human being is killed on our streets!"*

- **Historical facts**

"15 years ago two people started this company with this old machine."
"100 years ago people only ate meat once a week on Sundays. Today it is three times the amount."

- **Statement of a famous person**

It can be emotional or funny.

"Einstein said that the biggest force in the Universe is compound interest."
JFK said: *"Don't ask what your country can do for you. Ask what you can do for your country."*

- **Current events / information**

"The president of the USA said yesterday that ..."

- **Question for the audience**

Involve your audience and make them think. Example: *"What would you do if you only had 6 more months to live?"*

- **A picture or cartoon**

A picture says more than a 1000 words. If you show a picture, you should be silent and give the audience time to think about it until they fully understand the meaning of the picture. A cartoon often has a funny character and this will start your presentation in a good and happy mood.

"Now the first thing you have to do is get a client's attention."

- **Involvement of your audience**

"I would like you to close your eyes for the next 60 seconds."

- **Statistics**

"Every 13 seconds there is a burglary in America."

- **Statement**

"Red peppers from Holland are being harvested from an artificial substance as a base soil and therefore are no longer considered healthy."

- **Unusual definitions**

People will remember them.

- **Comparisons**

Well chosen comparisons can have a very dramatic effect on the audience.

- **Games**

Before you start with your talk, ask the audience to participate in a game. Example: 2 people will get a task and they have to hand envelopes to all members of the audience that contain special messages.

> *Whatever you chose to do, be creative. If you open well, the whole presentation will go much smoother and people will remember it.*

Answering questions during a presentation

> *Always try to anticipate potential questions from the audience and have some answers prepared.*

Make a list of all possible and difficult questions that might come. The better you are prepared, the more professional you will appear.

Make sure that the person who asked the question doesn't have to feel ashamed if the question appears to be ridiculous. Give him praise for asking and value his remarks.

If you can't answer a question, admit it openly. Don't try to come up with a BS answer. Promise to get back to that person at a later point in time with the answer. Here is what you should do:

1. Listen well.
2. Pause so that you have enough time to think about the answer.
3. Show appreciation for the question.
4. Praise the person for giving you the question.
5. Make eye contact with the audience.
6. Give a short and concise answer.

Example: *"This is a very interesting question. Thank you that you asked this question. I am sure that others are also interested in hearing about it. The easiest way to answer your question is..."*

Too many questions during a presentation can bother the flow of the presentation. That is why I always say the following things in the beginning: *"Dear audience, I can imagine that you will have a lot of questions during the presentation. Most of these questions will be automatically answered during my talk. May I ask you to wait with all your questions until the very end of the presentation? You can always write them down and I will give you the opportunity at the end to ask all your open questions. Please only ask if you could hear or understand something acoustically."*

This way, you can do your presentation and you won't get interrupted by some annoying person who will destroy the flow and the mood.

Some topics can be iffy and if there is a critical or negative person in the audience who is constantly challenging your content, it can really destroy your whole presentation and its positive mood.

Some negative people can negatively influence other people who would have otherwise bought your product. It is clear that you will never get 100% approval from everyone in your audience.

My tip for that: Don't answer questions publicly and in front of everybody. Make them personal and only at the end with that critical person. This is what I usually say: *"If you have questions during my presentation, I am happy to answer them in person after my talk."* If you get the difficult question in private, it doesn't matter so much because the other person cannot negatively influence other people. This way you have it under control.

Answering questions from different types of people

During a presentation you will always get questions from all kinds of people. But the type of person who asks the question is always different. Here is a list of the possible types of people who will ask questions:

1. The aggressive type
2. The submissive type
3. The know-it-all type
4. The irrelevant type

5. The strange type
6. The unanswerable questions type
7. The multiple-question type
8. The stupid type

It is important that you have a strategy for each one of them so that they don't interrupt your presentation in a negative way and people stay motivated.

Sometimes one person can destroy everything with his questions. Here are some tips and strategies to deal with these different people:

• *The aggressive type*
Normally, the aggressive type has prepared his poisonous remarks already in his head some time in advance. He is just waiting for his opportunity to attack you. Here are the ways to deal with those kinds of people:

1. Ask him if he could please repeat the question. It doesn't work if the question is very short. But if he has given you a loaded aggressive question before, it usually is a lot less aggressive if he has to ask it again in a different way.

2. Try to put yourself into the emotional state of the person who is asking the question. Why is he even asking this question in the first place? What is his problem or his motivation? Never fight back aggressively. Then you have lost immediately. Use a statement of understanding like: *"I can understand how you must feel."* or *"I am very sorry to hear that."*. Make a suggestion and tell him that you would like to personally talk to him after the presentation and to see if you can help him to resolve this issue. Understand that if someone comes from a negative place that you cannot directly move him into a positive mood. You first must bring him into a neutral place.

3. In some rare cases there are people in the audience who have simply no good intentions and they want to destroy your talk at all cost. In a situation like this you must be the stronger person and either put him back into his place and let him know who is the boss or have him removed from the room altogether. Even if there is a negative mood for a while you cannot allow someone to control your talk. You will find out that you will get the support of your audience if you show strength with an "asshole". The other people will see that you are not to be messed around and they will give you a lot more respect.

• **The submissive type**

If someone is asking a question, he will draw the attention of the audience to himself. Some people feel uncomfortable to be in the spotlight.

Often they are very hesitant to ask the question. But it is important for you to recognize that each person or question has the same importance. It is just as important for that person as if the question came from a more self-confident person.

Make them feel good about asking a question and encourage them. You could say something like: *"Thank you so much for asking this question. You have mentioned a very important point."*

• **The know-it-all type**

This type usually has a very big ego and wants attention. They usually don't ask questions but make statements. Those kinds of people think they are experts in their field or make everyone believe that they are. When you get this type of person you should say: *"Oh, how nice that we have such an expert among us (rub their belly) so in that case you can confirm the statement from before. May I ask you for some further advice later on in case we are not quite sure?"*

The goal is to get him on your side. If he is positive, he will help convince the group. If not, he can destroy a lot with his behavior.

Often, this type wants to add statements to your presentation or he will interfere. In that case you must act otherwise he will take over. You could say: *"Thank you so much for your input. It is important that the others also get the opportunity to learn or to ask questions, agreed? But I am so happy that we have such an expert among us."*

• *Irrelevant questions*
Some people ask a lot of irrelevant questions. Don't get caught up in those questions. Ask him to better formulate his question. You must not allow those kinds of people to get too much time and attention. You must be in charge of the presentation and sometimes you must dismiss this person in the interest of everybody else.

• *The strange type*
Some people try to trick you by asking strange or weird questions. Ask control questions to find out what he wants to know exactly. You are only allowed to answer if you get a clear question. If this type doesn't stop, you must ignore him.

• *Unanswerable questions*
Sometimes you cannot answer all questions. In that case you must be honest and admit that you don't know the answer. If you try to fake it, your credibility will suffer.

• *Multiple questions*
If someone asks multiple questions at once, it is often the inability of that person to communicate properly. Often, those people are confused and are not sure about what they really want to ask. In that case focus only on one topic in his series of questions and only answer that one. If that person is important or a decision maker you must try to answer all questions in a logical order by taking them apart.

• *Stupid questions*
It is possible that you will get a stupid question. But for the person who is asking the question, it is not stupid. Try not to talk down on people like that.

Don't say things like: *"As I have just mentioned before in my presentation..."*. Maybe your explanation wasn't clear enough. Be patient with those people. Repeat the answer if necessary. Everyone has the right to ask questions and to understand the content. Unfortunately, not everybody is smart.

How to deal with different people effectively

Top speakers have the ability to understand the motivations of people and to recognize how other people are feeling at the moment. You must be able to develop a feeling for the group to understand where most people are emotionally at any point in time.

Even though 90% of the people are generally positive, there are always those who are testing you or who are a pain in the butt. Some people simply have a lot of negative thoughts in their minds and it is important that you will not lose your cool or concept because of those people.

In general, you should always answer questions this way:
1. Praise and recognition
2. Use question techniques and rhetoric to answer questions
3. Have objections prepared

> **Most people don't get enough recognition and if you will give a person who is initially negative some praise, you will get him on your side.**

Using praise and recognition are some of the strongest tools to win someone over.

By using techniques and rhetoric to answer questions you will be able to find out better what they really want to know or what their overall motivation is. You could ask: "How do you mean exactly?" This way you can control the outcome of the conversation much better.

There is a great rule to deal with difficult or critical questions or statements. Here it is:

> **If someone asks an emotional question, you must argue with facts.**
> **If someone comes with facts or details,**
> **you must counter with an emotional statement.**

- **Example 1:**

Statement from other person: *"All you care about is money!"* (Emotional statement)

Answer: *"I can understand your concerns but fact is that 95% of all the money that comes in is going directly into the project. 2% are for administration and only 3% are profits that split them three-ways. In the end there is exactly 1% left for me. If I only cared about the money, then I should have changed the industry a long time ago."* (All facts)

- **Example 2:**

Statement from other person: *"You said that 95% of the money goes into the project. I don't understand why you spent $2 million on administration."* (All facts)

Answer: *"My dear Mr. Smith, without administration nothing works. In the end it is important that we can do our part to make the world a better place. If we didn't do that then more 50 people would be without a job and the state would have less taxes. I think that our project does a lot of good things for the community and makes a lot of lives better. Don't you think so, too?"* (Emotional answer)

Practice makes perfect

I was blessed to be able to co-teach my first seminar with my father at the age of 14 years of age. I was helping him to teach foreign managers to learn German with a new kind of learning technique.

When I was 22 years old I started training new sales people first in smaller groups and later on for bigger groups of more than 60 people. At first the trainings were one hour and later I gave seminars that lasted 3 days and were 8 hours each day. I have given a lot of seminars and I have had great moments but I also had terrible moments when everything went wrong.

> *Like everything in life there is always a learning curve and you must make certain mistakes in order to get better.*

Don't ever think that you already know everything. Still after years of giving seminars and courses I took a presentation training course in Hong Kong for two days and I was surprised how much new and better things I could learn. I thought I was good but I found out that I still had a lot of room for improvement!

A presentation is nothing else than a conversation

Most people think that they must somehow behave differently once they are in front of a large group of people. They change their behavior, the way their talk and their posture. This makes people believe that you are a completely different person than you actually are.

A presentation is much better and much more natural if you imagine that you are simply talking to a friend or a small group of friends. Your posture is more relaxed and your voice is totally normal. You are not nervous at all because there is no reason to be nervous. The whole thing is a lot less acted and more honest and people will recognize that.Don't try to be someone you are not. Just act normal and you will be surprised how much better your overall presentation will be.

> *Giving a presentation is nothing more than having a simple conversation.*

KISS – Keep it short and simple (and stupid)

The goal of each presentation is to get a certain message across. It is an art to take a complicated subject and to present in such a way that it is simple and easy to understand.

Try to explain things in a simple manner so that everybody will get it. The simpler your message, the more likely people will listen to you and understand the content. Do this every time even if you believe to have a room full of doctors or PhDs.

Authenticity

Be yourself and don't act differently. A presentation will come across as artificial if you think that you must change your normal behavior. If you give a presentation you are trying to convey trust so that your statements will be accepted. But you can only develop trust if people get the feeling that you are real.

No one needs a stereotype in presentations. It is about you and your individuality. If the true you comes across, people will appreciate it much more because they understand who they are dealing with.

Make longer pauses

Most people rush through their presentations and move way too fast when it would be important that the audience gets enough time to let the information sink in. Give your audience more time by making longer pauses.

> *Pauses bring up emotions.*
> *If you pause at the right point and you just made a certain statement,*
> *it will go much deeper under the other person's skin.*

You give people the possibility to think about it and to develop pictures in their heads. It is not about giving as much information as possible. You must make sure that you can the most important points across and then get them emotionally involved with those main points.

Make eye contact with everyone in your audience

In order to win your audience you must connect with each person. If you make eye contact with everyone even if it takes a while, you will make the whole thing much more personal.

This can be a challenge if you have a large group of people. Try to connect with three or four people each time you make a short pause. You will be surprised how much more involved people will be if they feel that you want to connect with them.

The opening and the closing of your presentation must be great

> *In the beginning you need to get the attention of your audience*
> *by having a strong opening. But when you finish,*
> *you should also have a strong or surprising end.*

People will remember the last statement or action that you will do and this will have an influence of the overall success of your presentation.

The last statement will be the one statement that people will remember even days after the presentation. That is why you should also think very hard about how you want to end your presentation.

The right and the wrong way to present a Power Point Presentation

Most slides contain way too much information.
The presentation might look professional and complete
but if the speaker is doing nothing else than reading off the slides
and going through each bullet point, the presentation is dead boring.

The meaning of the presentation is totally useless because people could take the presentation and read it alone at home. And nothing is worse than a boring presentation or meeting where you fall asleep and want to shoot yourself out of boredom.

Here a few tips to make it more interesting:
• Instead of using long texts and explanations on your slides you should only use short bullet points or pictures on each slide.
• You can take a bullet point and then explain in detail what you want to say. Never ever write everything on the slide and then read it to the audience.
• Use more pictures rather than too much text. These will create more emotions.
• Be creative and use surprising effects. If a presentation has "life", the attention is much greater.
• Also add empty pages or neutral pages into your presentation to move from one topic to another and to separate them better.
• Ask your audience a question and then wait before you continue with your slide. Pause and then show them the next slide. Don't just give away the answers by moving slides too fast.

Timing

If you focus on the main statements and the right structure you don't have to worry too much about time. But in case you must fill a longer period of time, you should always have a few extra things planned. Only use the extra information or tools if necessary.

You don't have to do everything. If the group gets it and the information came across the right way, you don't necessarily have to force them all of your material onto them. Sometimes it is much better to focus on the mood of the group even if you only have a small number of slides but a good conversation with your audience. Always ask yourself what is really important. Some topics will require more time than you had originally thought but if you skip it, your group will not follow.

Nervousness

Some people prefer death to public speaking. Some people get so nervous that their voice changes and their behavior is totally unnatural.

> *By being nervous you will only hurt yourself*
> *and diminish the effectiveness of your message.*
> *Later, you will beat yourself up over your own behavior.*

Here a few tips to calm down:
• It is totally normal that you can feel in increase in your pulse before an important presentation. Some of the most experienced speakers go through this each time. But as soon as you realize that you are getting nervous you should catch yourself and then take a moment to think about it. I always say to myself: *"There is absolutely no reason to be nervous. If I am nervous I will destroy everything. Stop it now and give them a good show. It is no problem at all. I have mastered much harder situations in life. This is ridiculous. So, go out there and give your best."*

• Also ask yourself what your mental attitude in regards to this topic is. Be clear about how you personally think about it. Are you totally 100% behind your statements? If you are convinced of the content yourself then there is no reason to be nervous. Make it aware to yourself that you believe in your message.

• Preparation, planning and practice can help to overcome the fear of public speaking. If you are well prepared then nothing can really go wrong. And if something unexpected happens, then simply go back to your content.

Realize that people want you to succeed

Audiences want you to be interesting, stimulating, informative and entertaining. They're rooting for you. People go to a seminar or a presentation and take out their time to see you.

Always expect a positive group that wants to learn something new. Always put yourself in their shoes and ask yourself what you would expect if you were in the audience.

You are there to help them, to teach them and to improve their lives. Anybody else is not welcome anyway. So there is nothing to worry about anyway.

Be energetic

Speaking to large audiences requires you to be a more energetic version of yourself. Project your voice, sound excited, and make sure your passion for the topic comes through.

The more energy you have, the more engaged the audience will be, and if you're excited, your audience will get excited. But if you're lame and boring, there's a good chance your audience will also be bored.

• **Be Entertaining**

Speeches should be entertaining and informative. I'm not saying you should act like a dancing monkey when giving a serious presentation. But unlike an e-mail or article, people expect some appeal to there emotions. Simply reciting dry facts without any passion or humor will make people less likely to pay attention.

• **Have Fun**

With a little practice you can inject your passion for a subject into your presentations.

Enthusiasm is contagious.

Tell a story

All presentations should tell a narrative that includes a beginning middle, and end. The first part of your presentation should always present the problem; ask yourself, *"what are we going to solve today?"* The middle of the presentation should present your key findings, but they should always tie back into the central issue you want to solve.

**By the end of the presentation,
your audience should feel like they've learned something,
and that they have a better understanding of the solution.**

Speeches are about stories. If your presentation is going to be a longer one, explain your points through short stories, quips and anecdotes.

Great speakers know how to use a story to create an emotional connection between ideas for the audience.

Project your voice

Nothing is worse than a speaker you can't hear. Even in the high-tech world of microphones and amplifiers, you need to be heard. Projecting your voice doesn't mean yelling, rather standing up straight and letting your voice resonate on the air in your lungs rather than in the throat to produce a clearer sound.

Put yourself in the audience

When writing a speech, see it from the audience's perspective. What might they not understand? What might seem boring?

Use WIIFM (What's In It For Me) to guide you.

Don't read off the charts. This one is a no brainer, but somehow Power Point makes people think they can get away with it. If you don't know your speech without cues, that doesn't just make you more distracting. It shows you don't really understand your message; a huge blow to any confidence the audience has in you.

Pay attention to design

Power Point and other presentation packages offer all sorts of ways to add visual "flash" to your slides: fades, swipes, flashing text, and other annoyances are all too easy to insert with a few mouse clicks.

Avoid the temptation to dress up your pages with cheesy effects and focus instead on simple design basics:

- **Use a sans serif font for body text**

  Sans serifs like Arial, Helvetica, or Calibri tend to be the easiest to read on screens.

- **Use decorative fonts only for slide headers, and then only if they're easy to read**

  Decorative fonts –calligraphy, German blackface, futuristic, psychotic handwriting, flowers, art nouveau, etc. – are hard to read and should be reserved only for large headlines at the top of the page. Better yet, stick to a classy serif font like Georgia or Baskerville.

- **Put dark text on a light background**

  Again, this is easiest to read. If you must use a dark background – for instance, if your company uses a standard template with a dark background – make sure your text is quite light (white, cream, light grey, or pastels) and maybe bump the font size up two or three notches.

- **Align text left or right**

  Centered text is harder to read and looks amateurish. Line up all your text to a right-hand or left-hand baseline – it will look better and be easier to follow.

- **Avoid clutter**

  A headline, a few bullet points, maybe an image – anything more than that and you risk losing your audience as they sort it all out.

CHAPTER 7

CREATING A
SALES SCRIPT

The money making machine = your sales script

> *Become a master in presenting.*
> *It is the one skill that can make you very successful.*

Even though most sales people have a variety of products that they can sell, there are usually one or two main products that they are mainly selling and that give them their main income.

Those core products are typically sold the same way or in the same manner. They have a sales approach and a sales script that is always the same and that is very effective. This sales script is built up logically and the whole process helps the sales person to make a sale on a regular basis.

In my six-year position as a financial advisor in Europe I mainly sold a retirement savings insurance plan that had a good commission structure and that was very popular at the time.

I developed a sales approach that was always the same and because I had perfected my sales script so much, my closing rate was more than 90%. There was even a time for nine months were I had a 100% closing rate because of my script.

During my six years I had perfected my sales script so much that I taught it to other sales people and when they used it, they were also successful with it. The sales script is the most important tool of a sales person and if done right it can make a lot of money over time.

Building a sales script

> *A sales script needs to be structured in a logical way.*
> *Start with a "problem", develop a need and present the solution.*

Building a sales script is not done in one day. It is a tool that must be developed and perfected over time. It must be structured logically and should not leave any questions unanswered. If there are potential objections you need to include arguments so that those objections won't even come up.

You need to mention difficult features or things in the beginning so that they won't come up later and won't matter so much anymore. And because you mentioned them early on and honestly, clients will trust you more and your credibility goes up.

It is crucial that you write down your entire script and learn it by heart. But when you are with a client it cannot sound fake or rehearsed. But your sentences and questions must be perfectly prepared and applied.

> *Everything that you say has a purpose.*
> *It should either create an emotion or matter later on in your script.*

Don't just talk aimlessly. Everything you say has a reason and must help you in the process.

You will need two or three possible versions to deal with the same objections. You need to write down all possible objections that anyone could ever bring up and then have several different answers ready. You need to be so well prepared that nothing can surprise you anymore. You will have an answer for absolutely anything.

I knew my sales script so well that you could have woken me up in the middle of the night and I could have recited it backwards in Chinese if you had asked me. (Just kidding)

The main reason why you must know your script by heart is because you need to be able to focus 100% of your energy on the behavior of the client. You need to be able to read signals and know when to change the course of the conversation. If you are focused on what you have to say next, you will not be able to read your client.

Good sales people have their script down to a T so that they don't have to worry about it anymore. All you need to worry about is the behavior and the energy of your client.

> *Since most people are visually oriented, you should use a lot of sketches and pictures to explain things. The most important thing is to create a logical, clear and simple structure.*

The two-step sales approach and pre-selling

> *Ask a lot of questions in the beginning and analyze exactly what your client wants to achieve.*

When I was working as a financial planner back in Europe we used to have two appointments per client.

The first appointment was to present the service and sell the USP (Unique Selling Proposition = what makes your company special). During that meeting we would also fill out a questionnaire with the client.

The main goal was to gather all the information about his financial situation so that we could analyze it back at the office and then make recommendations in the second meeting. Another crucial factor was to do pre-selling. This means that I would ask questions like this:

"I can see that you have your car insurance with insurance company ABC. Assuming I could find a cheaper and better solution for you, would you be willing to look at it?"
(General opening question)

"What if you really liked it and felt that it was the better choice, would you be willing to change your car insurance?"
(Pre-closing question)

"So can I take this as one of my jobs for next time to present you with a better solution?"
(Pre-closing question)

"You have $100,000 in your savings account and it only has a performance of 1.5% per year. Do you think that is a good annual performance for your money?"
(General opening question)

"What if I could show you a solution where you could have 7% per year but still a very safe type of investment, would you be interested in that?"
(General opening question)

"Would you be willing to make changes so that you can make more money in the years to come?"
(Pre-closing question)

"It is really important to save for your retirement. As far as I can see today, you don't have any kind of savings plan for that purpose yet. As you know, there are more old people than young people in our current society and the state will not be able to provide you with enough money when you retire. Do you think it is important or even necessary to do something about that?"
(General opening question)

"What if I had some great and fantastic solutions where you could also save on your taxes at the same time?"
(General opening question)

"Would you be willing to take a closer look at that?"
(General opening question)

"Would you be willing to act on it, too?"
(Pre-closing question)

"Great, then I take this as my order from you to present you with a retirement savings plan solution for our second meeting, ok?"
(Pre-closing question)

Pre-selling is one of the most powerful ways to sell. At the current moment you are not selling anything and the client knows that. That is why he is relaxed. But you prepare him for what will come in the second meeting and you ask questions to open him up for possible solutions.

> *If he says yes to you during some pre-selling questions, then half of your sale is already done.*

Pre-selling is key in the two-step approach. You can explain a few things in general but you don't actually mention any specific products or companies. You ask the client general questions to see if he is open for a specific topic and to make a change. If he says yes, you ask a second and third question to make sure that you can present him with an offer in your second meeting. It is also very important that you create a lot of curiosity during your first meeting and don't give away too much information.

> *The more curious a client is the better. You need to build him up during the first meeting so that he can't wait for the second meeting.*

The second meeting is fairly easy if you did a good job in your initial meeting. Typically, you start with a list of goals that he selected the last time. And then you present him with solutions that will help to achieve those financial goals. If you did your pre-selling well, you can easily present him with solutions (= financial products) that you mentioned in the first meeting.

Building rapport in the beginning

> *Never get straight to the point in the beginning. Focus on the relationship, on building rapport and developing a positive mood.*

During the first few minutes you need to focus on the client. Do a lot of small talk and ask a lot of questions. Ask the client about his day and hobbies. Show honest interest in your client. The main goal is to develop rapport and that the client likes you.

You cannot start with your sales presentation if you don't have a good foundation where there is a positive mood and everybody likes each other. If there is something troubling your client, he won't be able to give you his full attention and in that case it would not be wise to start with the sales presentation. Before you begin talking about your product, you should ask a few questions first.

1. *"Since last time that we have met, did anything change in your personal situation?"*
2. *"The first time that we met, you told me that you three main goals were to "invest wisely", "save taxes" and "save for a down payment for your house". Are those goals still the same?"*
3. *"In our first meeting you asked me to show you some options for an investment that has a great return but it is still safe at the same time. Are you still open to find out what that is?"*

"Great, then I am happy to start with my presentation."

The reason why you should ask these questions is to find out if anything changed that could hinder him to make a buying decision. Sometimes people read something in the newspaper or on the Internet and it changes their whole attitude.

It is also possible that someone had a major event happen in his or her life like for example a car accident where the car was totaled and the client needs to use his money to buy a new car first before he can make any kinds of investments.

I have seen new sales people talk for an hour only to find out that the client knew from the beginning that he wouldn't buy the product. A situation like this can be very frustrating and is a waste of time for everyone involved. One quick question in the beginning would have been wiser.

Building trust and giving something first

Always do something for your client first.
Then he or she will feel the need to reciprocate by signing your deal.

It is important to give your client some sort of advantage, value or great advice in the beginning. You need to show him that you really care about his personal situation and that your goal is not just to sell him your product. Example: *"Mr. Client, I have looked at your paperwork and found that you are over insured in two areas. If you make an small adjustment, you will save $200 per year."*

Even though it's a small thing and you don't make any money with it, you'll make him happy and build trust. Most people will later return the favor by signing a contract because they felt that you helped them earlier.

The carpet sales people from the Middle East know this technique really well. When you walk past a carpet store, they try to talk to you and say something that grabs your attention. After they offer you a free drink or tea. Because most people don't want to appear rude, they accept the "free gift" and take the tea. And since you are already in the carpet store, they start showing you some really nice carpets.

You might not need a new carpet but because you feel a bit guilty because you received something for free, you consider buying a carpet. Some people spend $1000 because they got a free tea.

But if you don't actually have a gift or an advantage, you can also use praise and recognition. Most people don't get enough praise and recognition in their lives and everybody is craving it. If you give it out, your client will also feel the need to reciprocate. Tell him that his buying decision in the past was the right one and tell him that he made a really good choice.

Curiosity is key

In order to keep the attention high, you must always maintain a level of curiosity.

Don't tell your client what the product is in detail. You must always maintain a certain level or curiosity to keep his attention high. If you tell him everything, he will lose interest. And if he loses interest, you will lose the sale.

You must always keep a few things in the air. If you have two meetings, he must be excited and curious what to expect in the second meeting. You must always keep the curiosity at a high level.

Tell him things like: "Mr. Client, I can promise you this. I have a solution for you that will make you very happy. I won't give you any details now but you should be excited for our next meeting because you will save a lot of money!"

Summary of initial meeting

Focus on the goals and dreams of your client and connect your product with them.

Start with his dreams and goals. Make a list of his dreams and goals and then tell him that you will try your best to achieve those dreams and goals. For example, if you are a financial advisor, your client might have the following 5 dreams and goals:

1. Buy a new house
2. Save taxes
3. Go on a trip to Europe next year
4. Save money for retirement – no more worries about money later in life
5. Buy a red sports car

Before you start with your presentation, you must ask a few pre-closing questions like:
- *"Mr. Client, take a good look at your goals and dreams. Assuming I could help you to achieve those goals, would you be happy about it?"*
- *"Assuming I could show you products and solutions that would help you to achieve those goals, would you consider them?"*
- *"Assuming those products were exactly what you needed to achieve your goals, would you take advantage of them?"*

"Ok, great, then let's find out exactly HOW we can do that!"

You start with his most important goals and always keep coming back to those goals. The goals are your reference point and they should motivate your client. Basically, the goals will become one with your product because your product will make sure that he will achieve his goals.

Always start with praise and recognition. You can also bring a small gift or surprise to create a positive mood in the beginning.

It is important that you smile and laugh a lot. If you do that, your client cannot help but to smile as well.

Smiling and laughing is contagious and if the whole sales presentation is done in a positive mood, your client will connect positive feelings when it comes to your product and company. His brain will actually produce endorphins (= the happy hormones).

It should be a happy moment and the overall mood is crucial to your success.

The structure of a sales script for a second meeting

> ***Start with a problem. Make it emotional and painful.***
> ***The logical conclusion to solve that problem is your product.***

Make an analysis of the client's situation. Find out exactly what he wants. Find out what motivates him and where he could have a deficit / problem.

- *"Mr. Client, can you remember what we talked about in our initial meeting?"*
- *"What exactly do you still have remembered?"* (Control question)
- *"I have summarized your goals and dreams for you again. Did anything change or are they still the same?"* (Control question)
- *"In our last meeting you told me that you wanted to invest $20,000 in such a way that it is safe but still has a great performance. Is that still the case? Is $20,000 still ok to invest?"* (Use specific number that you have defined in the first meeting)
- *"Well, Mr. Client, if I were able to show you a product that fulfills your requirements exactly, would you take advantage of it and invest the money?"* (Pre-closing question)
- *"Well, then let me explain..."*

> ***It is important to ask these questions in the beginning***
> ***to find out if anything has changed.***

You will also be able to read his reaction when you ask him the pre-closing questions and you will know if he is ready to buy or if you need to do more convincing during your presentation. You will feel if he might come up with objections or critical questions.

> ***Don't be afraid to ask those questions early. You can only win.***

Creating a deficit and making him aware of a problem

A client will only buy if he sees a NEED to buy (problem or deficit). If he feels that he has no problem, he will not buy anything.

The main goal of this part is to make the client AWARE of a potential situation or problem.

You need to describe a problem in an emotional manner and get under his skin. If your client believes that everything is just fine with this life, he will not develop the need to act.

You need to show him the problem and make him aware of the problem. You need to show him a situation that is bad or that could go bad in the future. You can also show him a perfect example of how things should be and then compare it with his current still imperfect situation.

Example: A client believes that he has done everything to protect his family in case there is an accident and he would have to go on disability.

- *"Mr. Client, did you know that you would only get 60% of your last income? In your case this is $3000 per month."*
- *"Honestly, do you really think that you could still have a good life with $3000 per month?"*
- *"What would that mean for your family?"*
- *"What would you have to give up and where would you have to cut back? What could you or one of your family members no longer do?"*
- *"You see, an old-time friend of mine was exactly in the same situation. He had an accident and his back was badly hurt. He spent months in the hospital."*
- *"His back pain became a chronic pain and he had to stop working."*
- *"His family was affected by it in a big way. They had to move from a big and nice house into a small depressing apartment."*
- *"His wife ended up leaving him and he fell into a depression."*
- *"Is this really what you would want for your family, too?"*
- *"He could have prevented all of this with a policy for $100 per month."*

All of a sudden your client will develop a lot of emotions and fears. The more detail you can give him, the better he can picture the story. Use several examples of how bad the situation could get and then show him one product that could take care of all of the problems.

Using control questions

Control questions will help you to see if the client really understood what you just talked about so that you can move on to the next topic.

> *You can only get tot he next topic if you are sure that the client "got it". If not, you must go back and explain it again.*

After you have done your entire presentation, you should summarize the most important points. This is the phase when you will go into the end phase: the closing phase.

But before you can do that, you need to make sure that your client or audience really understood everything and agreed with everything. If you jump the gun too early, you will have objections and people still need to think about it.

Let's say that you covered 5 main topics. If your client can agree with the conclusion of all of these 5 topics and you have the feeling that he has really understood those arguments, then you are ready to move into the final phase. Therefore, you must ask control questions and get a clear and convincing YES for each topic. Example:

- *"Mr. Client, let's summarize the most important points again."*
- *"Do you also agree that it is important to save for retirement?"*
- *"Do you see and agree that we will have a problem in the future if we don't save money?"*
- *"What would happen if you solely rely on the state and social security to take care of you?"*

He answers...

- "Ok, very well. Then I can cross off this topic from my list and we can both agree that it makes sense to save for your retirement, right? Yes."
- "Ok, let's move to the next point..."

Once you are convinced that the client "got it", you can move forward. If you see that he is still struggling with one topic, it gives you the chance to talk about it and explain it further.

Another great way to see if your client really listened and understood what you had to say is to change roles. This is how it goes: "Mr. Client, let's switch roles right now. I am your client and you are the advisor. Let's play a little game. Please explain to me why this product makes sense."

I have done this on several occasions and it always went well. The client actually sells the product to himself. He gives himself all the reasons why it is good for him. Another way to go into the closing phase is the following strategy;

- "Mr. Client, let's summarize the most important points again."
- "I have made five sketches and explained a different situation each time. "
- "Can you please summarize for me what we just talked about on these five sketches?"
- "Which one of these problems gives you the biggest stomachache?"
- "What could be done to fix this problem?"
- "Assuming I actually had the perfect solution for you that could not only solve this one big problem but also the other four, how would that sound?"
- "Wouldn't that be great?"
- "Well, it is your lucky day. Let's have a look..."

Product presentation

**Your product must be the ideal solution for the problem.
The actual product should only be revealed at the very end.**

The features of the product are the solution for the problem and the name or type of the product is almost irrelevant. It is important what it can do for the client to help him solve his problem. The brand name or type is not that important. I often covered the actual name of the company who provided the product. I wanted to client to focus on the problem and make him realize that this product would be the right solution regardless of the company who stood behind it.

Often, I took the offer off the table and put it back in my bag. Depending on the client's reaction, you could see that he wanted it even more because I took it away from him.

Explaining something with a drawing or a sketch

> *Use a lot of sketches and drawings to explain important points. People understand visuals much better then just words.*

The best way to explain things is to draw. When you draw and explain at the same time, your client will be able to understand your argument better. Most people are visually oriented and if you can use two senses (words and visuals) you will be much more effective.

I always have a number of logical drawings in my repertoire to make a certain point. If you use drawings in your sales presentation, half of the sale is already done. Use it for your main arguments or points and the client will be convinced.

Tell a story

All sales presentations should tell a narrative that includes a beginning middle, and end. The first part of your presentation should always present the problem; ask yourself, "what are we going to solve today?"

The middle of the presentation should present your key findings, but they should always tie back into the central issue you want to solve.

By the end of the presentation, your client should feel like he has learned something, and that he has a better understanding of the solution.

Sales scripts can be presented as a story.

If your presentation is going to be a longer one, explain your points through short stories, quips and anecdotes. Great sales people know how to use a story to create an emotional connection between the product and the client.

> *A story is always emotional and entertaining.*
> *Most people love stories because they loved them when they were*
> *little childrenand they understand the message much better.*

Be energetic and excited

You don't need any sales techniques or scripts if you are passionate and excited about your product. The more energy you have, the more engaged will be your client, and if you're excited, your client will also get excited. But if you're lame and boring, there's a good chance your client will also be bored.

Be entertaining – your presentation should be entertaining and informative. Don't act like a dancing monkey when giving a serious presentation but show some emotions. Simply reciting dry facts without any passion or humor will make people less likely to pay attention.

> *Enthusiasm is contagious.*

KISS – Keep it short and simple (and stupid)

> *The goal of each presentation is to get a certain message across.*
> *It is an art to take a complicated subject and to present in such a way*
> *that it is simple and easy to understand for everyone.*

Try to explain things in a simple manner so that everybody will get it. The simpler your message, the more likely people will listen to you and understand the content. Do this every time even if you believe to have a room full of doctors or PhDs. Don't overcomplicate things because you want to look good. If you lose the client because he doesn't understand what you are talking about, it won't help you to make a sale.

The client gets bored and the attention is going down

> *When you feel that the mood is going down*
> *or the client gets bored, you must add some laughter.*

Sometimes it can happen that you are so focused on your own presentation that you don't realize that you are losing the client. This happens when you talk too much and make a monologue.

Most people listen to you only out of politeness but because you have bored them with too many unimportant things, they have turned off their brain. In that case, you must do or say something that will shake him up. Typically, tell a story or make a joke. Change the subject. Stop what you are doing and ask the client a question.

Continuing with your program doesn't make sense because you will not win over the client anyway.

Closing phase and signing the contract

Closing is easy and logical if you did your job well before.

It is crucial that you can create emotions and curiosity in a sales script.

Before you show him the actual product, you should go back to the beginning and make a summary. Go back to his goals and dreams. Check off each goal and dream one by one. Once the entire list is checked off, you can say the following things:

- _"Mr. Client, as you can see, we were able to check off all of your goals and dreams with this product."_
- _"What do you think about that? Isn't that great? Yes."_

Bring the most important arguments back and use the sketches to illustrate them again. Then say:

- _"Wow, this is really incredible. We can solve all of these problems with one solution."_
- _"But there is a catch..."_

You must make your client excited, happy and relieved. You can see and feel that he is ready to buy. If you did your job well, there should be no objections. Most of the objections should have been answered in your presentation.

Some people like to ask about three questions that your client will answer with a YES before they ask the final question for the order. In my experience it is ok to ask those questions but make sure that they don't sound too rehearsed. It is better to create a logical bridge that flows into the contract.

Never say: _"Do you want to sign the contract or not?"_ (This will kill your deal.)

I often say: *"Everything sounds great but there is a catch!"* Then I pause and wait for the client's reaction.

He will respond: *"What is it?"*

I say: *"Not everyone can do it."*

He will say: *"Why not? Can I do it?"*

My answer: *"We will have to find out. First, we need to submit an application and then we will know if you will get accepted."*

Of course, depending on the product that is not always possible or necessary. But it is fun to see how much the client actually wants the deal in the end. Also, instead of saying: *"Do you want to sign the deal?"* You could give him the choice between two options: *"Do you prefer the red one or the blue one?"*

And finally, simply take out the contract from your suitcase and start filling out the details. Don't ask whether he wants the deal. Simply assume that he wants it.

> ## It is crucial that you create a positive mood BEFORE you go into the closing phase.

I often make a little joke or tell a story before I start with contract. Most contracts are written very dry and are very technical. Never let the client read the contract in detail. It will kill the positive mood and arguments because the company will always try to protect itself. So in general a contract is never a positive thing for the client.

I often say: *"Mr. Client, the contract summarizes what we just talked about. Obviously, there is a lot of legal language in the contract and we can't change anything anyway. So if you are happy with the things that I just explained to you, then please sign right here."*

If the client insists and wants to know the details of the contract, then I will do it together with him and explain each step in an easy language. I make sure that he is not left alone with the contract and could get scared and then change his mind.

I simply say things like:

- "And this point is what we just talked about earlier..."
- "Here the company needs to protect itself against unfair clients, which makes perfect logical sense..."
- "And this point is the guarantee I mentioned before..."

Securing the deal and preparation for future deals

Nothing is worse than spending hours with a client to close a sale and then to have it revoked the very next day. After the deal has been signed you must secure it and in case there might be any doubt, you must try to eliminate them.

One strategy is to ask the following question at the very end after the client signed the deal: *"Mr. Client, why did you just sign this contract?"*

At this point, he should give you several arguments why he did it.

> **The goal is that he sells the product to himself again and is more convinced.**

After this, another question: "Mr. Client, now imagine you are all happy and you go to work tomorrow. During your coffee break you talk to your work colleague and you tell him about this deal. Your friend says to you: "Oh my God, how could you have been so stupid? This was a huge mistake!" How are you going to counter and what are you going to tell him?"

The goal is to secure the deal and make sure that he is prepared for people who might try to change his mind or influence him. Some people will do a deal with you because they are easily influenced. But the problem is also that another person (or even your competition) could easily influence them, too.

Main objection: "I need to think about it."

> *Don't ever accept a "no" or "I have to think about it".*
> *There is nothing to think about. Either he does it now*
> *or you must help him to understand all the advantages of your product.*

Do not leave his house before you have completely eliminated all possible questions. There should be nothing left open or unsure.

When it comes to investments, for example, the question in the end is whether he will invest or not. But it should not be whether he will invest or not AND if he should do $20,000 or $30,000.

The question of how much must be answered and you must make that decision together with the client. In case of doubt, chose the lower amount so that he can do for sure.

> *A lot of sales people make the mistake that*
> *they also offer 2 different products at the same time.*

Now imagine if you were the client. You need to decide between product A and B, whether to invest $20,000 or $30,000 and you are not sure if you want to invest in the first place. So basically, there are 3 BIG OPEN QUESTION MARKS in the room.

Of course, he cannot make a decision. It is too much for him. There are too many factor left open to decide. If he is not an expert in financial matters anyway, he is unsure to begin with.

You absolutely MUST define every little detail and make a decision on it. There should be no more questions or points to decide. All that he needs to think about is whether he will do it or not. But all the other details must be clear.

When people tell me that they have to think about it, it is usually one of three things:

1. It is an excuse because he doesn't want to do it. (Doesn't see the need, doesn't have the money or is afraid of confrontation)

2. He is unsure about too many factors.

3. There is another reason that he is not telling you and you must find out what it is by asking questions.

In that case I typically say: *"Mr. Client, can we please be really honest for a moment? What is the real problem?"* (And then wait for his answer...)

Position yourself as an expert and say something complicated

You must position yourself as an expert and not as a sales person. Once in a while say something complicated about the product or the industry to gain more trust and credibility.

This is a technique that I have used a lot. Basically, when you are talking to another person, you are tying to gain his trust. But it is not with facts and smart words that you will convince another person. It happens all on an emotional level. I call this level the Neanderthal level.

Imagine that your client who is typically rational and logical has a big huge Neanderthal sitting on his shoulder. This Neanderthal is not very smart. But he is very emotional. If you can "convince" the Neanderthal who is much bigger and stronger than the rational person, then you will win over the client.

For one, two or sometimes even five minutes I will explain something that is very technical. I use a lot of technical terms that no one understands. I know for a fact that my client will not be able to follow me.

But the main reason why I do this is to win over the Neanderthal. The client will think the following things: *"...I really don't understand what he just told me. But I think this guy really knows his stuff and is an expert. That is why I can trust him..."*

The content of explaining something in a technical manner is not important. Important is that the client will get the feeling that you are very competent and that he can trust you.

Using a power point presentation

> ### A Power Point Presentation
> ### can be a great tool to structure a sales presentation.

When creating a sales presentation you have to see it from the audience's perspective. What might they not understand? What might seem boring? Use WIIFM (What's In It For Me) to guide you. Don't read off the charts. A presentation is a helping tool and it should only have pictures, facts, charts, statements or other things that support your message. It should never have a lot of text. Too much text is boring and someone could simply read the slides and then you would not be necessary.

Even though you have a structure and charts, it is only a guideline. It is only the main thread. You must be able to deviate from the presentation and if necessary only use key charts to make a point. Sometimes all you need is two or three slides to explain something and make a sale.

Most slides contain way too much information. The presentation might look professional and complete but if the speaker is doing nothing else than reading off the slides and going through each bullet point, the presentation is dead boring. The meaning of the presentation is totally useless because people could take the presentation and read it alone at home. And nothing is worse than a boring presentation or meeting where you fall asleep and want to shoot yourself out of boredom.

Here a few tips to make it more interesting:

• Instead of using long texts and explanations on your slides you should only use short bullet points or pictures on each slide.

• You can take a bullet point and then explain in detail what you want to say. Never ever write everything on the slide and then read it to the audience.

• Use more pictures rather than too much text. These will create more emotions.

• Be creative and use surprising effects. If a presentation has "life", the attention is much greater.

• Also add empty pages or neutral pages into your presentation to move from one topic to another and to separate them better.

• Ask your audience a question and then wait before you continue with your slide. Pause and then show them the next slide. Don't just give away the answers by moving slides too fast.

How to deal with different people effectively

Top sales people have the ability to understand the motivations of people and to recognize how other people are feeling in the moment. You must be able to develop a feeling for the client to understand where he emotionally stands at any point in time.

Even though most people are generally positive, there are always those who are testing you or who are a pain in the butt.

Some people simply have a lot of negative thoughts in their minds and it is important that you will not lose your cool or concept because of those people.

In general, you should always answer questions this way:

1. Praise and recognition
2. Use question techniques and rhetoric to answer questions
3. Have objections prepared

Most people don't get enough recognition and if you will give a person who is initially negative some praise, you will get him on your side.

> ### *Using praise and recognition are some of the strongest tools to win someone over.*

By using techniques and rhetoric to answer questions you will be able to find out better what they really want to know or what their overall motivation is. You could ask: *"How do you mean exactly?"* This way you can control the outcome of the conversation much better.

There is a great rule to deal with difficult or critical questions or statements. Here it is:

> ### *If someone asks an emotional question, you must argue with facts. If someone comes with facts or details, you must counter with an emotional statement.*

- **Example 1:**

Statement from other person: *"All you care about is money!"*

(Emotional statement)

Answer: *"I can understand your concerns but fact is that 95% of all the money that comes in is going directly into the project. 2% are for administration and only 3% are profits that split them three-ways. In the end there is exactly 1% left for me. If I only cared about the money, then I should have changed the industry a long time ago."*

(All facts)

- ***Example 2:***

Statement from other person: *"You said that 95% of the money goes into the project. I don't understand why you spent $2 million on administration."*
(All facts)

Answer: *"My dear Mr. Smith, without administration nothing works. In the end it is important that we can do our part to make the world a better place. If we didn't do that then more 50 people would be without a job and the state would have less taxes. I think that our project does a lot of good things for the community and makes a lot of lives better. Don't you think so, too?"*
(Emotional answer)

Practice makes perfect

> *Like everything in life there is always a learning curve and you must make certain mistakes in order to get better.*

Don't ever think that you already know everything. You must have as many different sales situations as possible to get better.

Sometimes young sales people ask me to close a "bigger fish" because they are scared to lose the business due to their inexperience. In that case I always refuse even though we most likely will lose the business due to his inexperience.

I tell the young sales person the following thing: *"How do you think I was able to close bigger fish? At one point I was also inexperienced and I needed to lose a few bigger fish so that I could LEARN how to close a bigger fish in the future. If you try to avoid the sales lesson and always use your manager with bigger clients, you will never grow into a great sales person. You must screw up a few deals to realize what is really important and what to do better next time."*

CHAPTER 8

GREAT
CLOSING
TECHNIQUES

There is really no need to close

If there is TRUST closing is easy.

Top sales people never have to "close" the sale in the real sense of the word. If the presentation was so solid that there was no need to close. The sale was a done deal even before the sales person set foot into the prospect's office.

Closing is one the basic elements of selling. But in my opinion, closing is a logical consequence when you develop a good relationship, build trust and if the client can see the need for the product. Often, people don't close the sale because they made some mistakes in the beginning or during the presentation. Usually, they didn't read the signs in the client's behavior or didn't focus on the relationship.

If you have problems closing, then you should focus on how to build trust, how to get the client to like you more, how to dress more professional and how to work on the way you talk to the client. In the end, closing is a logical consequence of a job well done. But if you need to have some ideas on how to ask for the order, then let this brochure give you some ideas and inspirations.

My personal closing rate

When I was a financial planner, I had a very high closing rate. Typically, it was between 80% and 90%. If there was anything to improve in my client's situation, I would usually be able to sell him a product.

For about nine months, I had a perfect closing rate of 100%. I simply didn't take "no" for an answer. Of course, this was also not typical but it shows that my mental attitude was very determined. I knew that when I walked in that door that the client had no more chance.

What were the reasons for such a high closing rate?

1. Of course, if you know your "stuff" well and you have great products to offer then it is hard to say no for any client.
2. But the main thing is trust, professionalism, feeling where the client is at emotionally and mental attitude.
3. If you have a lot of experience and self-confidence in your own abilities and knowledge, then you won't waste your time with someone who is not going to take advantage of what you have to offer. Basically, you won't even deal with people that don't have the potential to buy.

Identifying the client's motivation

It is difficult to know what exactly motivates a client. But this is exactly what you must find out to close a sale. You can ask a number of questions to understand and learn how your client thinks and what he wants.

Make a basic assessment how to take your client and then tell him what he wants to hear. Use his language and the goals that he mentioned during your presentation. In that case he cannot but say "yes" in the end.

Mental power for sales people

In life and business you often need courage and self-confidence. These things are not always easy to come by. As a sales person you are often confronted with rejection. Some people don't do well with rejection and it leads to them giving up or breaking on the inside.

There is only one thing that will counter that: clarity! Most people have no clarity in business and in life. They have no clear goals and they don't really know why they are doing what they are doing.

Selling is a means to an end. It helps you to reach your personal goals. So find out first what it is that you want from life. Set goals and get clarity. Do it on paper and leave nothing to chance.

Ask yourself why you go to work. If you had $10 million, tomorrow would you still go to work? And if yes, why? If not, how much money do you need to do something different or to stop working? If you do this, you will get further than you can imagine. Clarity will give you mental power and self-confidence.

Too much information and unnecessary facts

Decisions are always done on an emotional level. Even though you need facts and data to help with the decision, in the end it is always an emotional factor that determined whether someone bought a product or not.

The left side of our brain is responsible for facts, data, numbers and rational information. The right side will store pictures, memories and emotions.

In order to get big clients, you need to contact many clients and by the law of averages you will eventually have a big client in your portfolio. Getting big clients is a normal part of business but they are random and seldom. Out of 50 clients you will have one big one. But if you don't take the other 49 clients, you will fail miserably.

Dependency and independence

When it comes to closing it is also crucial how your mental state is as a sales person. If you are personally under financial pressure and you absolutely need to make a sale to earn the commission, your client can actually feel it. Most of the time and because he can feel it, he will not do the deal.

If you only focus on a few big clients hoping that you can close them, you put a lot of psychological pressure on you. But if you have many other possibilities or open clients, then there is no apparent pressure coming from you and it seems like you couldn't care less if one particular client says "yes" or "no" to your offer. And because you are more relaxed and not dependent on any one client, you are usually more successful. You will close more deals if your client doesn't feel like you need his commission urgently.

The same is true for dating. If you are running around like a horny wolf you will never get a girl. But if you are relaxed and even act as if you don't care or need it, you will be more successful in dating.

Credibility is key

The main factor in closing is trust. Everything you do or say will add trust and credibility or take it away.

If you have higher premiums than your competition, it is better to talk about it in the beginning. You can say something like: "Mr. Client, we are the most expensive provider of this product in our industry. But this has good reasons. Would you like to know what those reasons are?"

> *If your credibility is high, you are more likely to close.*
> *If it is low, closing gets harder.*

Understanding closing techniques is important, but there are no magic words to guarantee that you make the sale. You must start by helping your customer identify his needs and then demonstrating that your product or service offers an affordable solution that addresses those needs. With that foundation, a good closing will help you cement the deal and grow your business.

The logical conclusion

**If there are no more questions then the next step is to...
fill out the application.**

The logical conclusion is the most common type of closing technique. If you have done your job well before, then there should be no more questions or objections. You can simply go straight into filling out the contract: *"Do you still have any questions that we haven't covered? Does everything so far make sense? Well, then I suggest you should do it. Let's begin with the paperwork."*

Selection between two choices

Do you want the blue or the red model?

Instead of asking whether the client wants to do the deal with a closed question ("Do you want to do it? Yes or no?"), you give him the option between two choices. You don't ask him if he wants to do it and distract him by giving him two options.

If you ask a closed question, chances are that the client will say "no". By focusing on two choices, your client has to decide between two things and not if he wants to buy or not.

Invitational close

"Why don't you give it a try?"

The invitational close is one of the most successful closing techniques among top sales people. At the end of your presentation you simply say to the customer: "If you like what I just told you, why don't you give it a try?" Most people are inclined to answer with "ok". If you add a nice smile, it is hard to say no.

Assumptive close

> ### *"Please sign right here..."*

If you have an established relationship with the customer and he respects your judgment you don't have to ask him whether he wants to do the deal or not. You simply assume that he wants it. Don't ask. Go straight into order mode without asking for permission or approval. When the timing is right, put an X on the signature line, hand it to the customer and say, "Here", and then be quiet.

As long as the sales pro makes sure that he covers each step of the sales process and provides enough value to the customer, assuming that the sale will close is a powerful and highly effective closing technique. If you learn only one close, this is the one to learn.

Approval first close

> ### *"Let's see if you get approved..."*

With some products or services a client needs to be approved first. In reality, you fill out the entire application and the client signs the contract in the end.

But you don't say to him "You must sign the contract". Instead you say: *"Please confirm here that everything that you have told me is correct and the truth". "If we are lucky, you will get approved..."*

Depending on the company and the products, you already know that he will be approved but you tell him after the fact. Sometimes people don't even realize that they just signed a contract that is binding. They believe that they can still make the decision later on.

Free trial close

> **"Why don't you try it out for 30 days?**
> **If you don't like it, you can always send it back for a full refund."**

You let the customer try the product for free in the hopes the customer will fall in love with it or that he is too lazy to return it. Example: *"We'll give you the product free for your evaluation and only charge you if you don't return it."*

Car sales people will let you drive a brand new car for a day. It is hard to return a brand new car that looks great, smells nice, drives easily and then going back to the old beat up car.

The idea behind the free trial is that you will sell the product to yourself and that you don't want to return it.

Stories

> *Stories are great closing techniques*

Every kid loves stories and when we grow up and become adults, we still like them. Stories are a great way to sell and explain a product. We can relate to stories and the moral of the story will help us to make a decision.

If you can use a good story as a closing technique, chances are that you will make the sale.

- Are you interested in an idea that could make you thousands of dollars extra?
- Yes.
- Very well. The best way to explain it is by telling you a story...

Now you will have the full attention of your client.

The conclusion of the story should lead straight into the conclusion why the product is perfect for your customer and why he should buy right now.

Connecting with goals and dreams

> *"As you can see, we can reach all your goals*
> *and dreams with this one product..."*

At the beginning of your sales presentation you make a list of all the goals and dreams of your customer. Then you ask:

- What if I could show you a solution (product) that could help you to reach all those goals and dreams? Would you take advantage of the product if that were the case?
- Yes.
- Ok, then let me start to explain...

At the end of your presentation you summarize everything that you have talked about and you check off each item on this goal list.

- Mr. Client, we were able to check off all of your goals with this one product. Isn't that great?
- Yes.
- Well, then the next step is to fill out the paperwork. Do you want me to fill it out or do you want to take my pen?

Confirmation

"All I need now from you is for you to confirm that everything what you said is true and then we can get started right away."

Another way of saying it is: *"Then all I need you to do is to confirm right here that everything is true and correct like you just told me."*

Instead of saying: *"Do you want to buy the product or pay the price..."*, you switch it out with the word *"confirm"*. It is softer and confirming the truth is easy. But buying and paying is hard.

Where do you want to do the paperwork?

"Do you want me to send you the paperwork to your home or to your office?"

You don't ask if he wants to do the deal. You take the focus away from the actual yes-or-no question. You ask him where he wants to do it and then his focus is on either the office or his place at home.

Time pressure or deadline

> **"We must act in the next 24 hours or this opportunity is gone."**

This is one of the best techniques that I often use when selling stocks. Usually, there is an increase in price and you can only guarantee the price for a day or two.

This is important because it forces the client to make a decision now. Deadlines are very effective and people hate to lose an opportunity. Often, this is the only reason why they do it. They are afraid to pay more later or to lose the deal altogether. That becomes the main focus and the actual product is often secondary in the closing phase.

The reverse close

> **"Is there any reason why you wouldn't buy this product?"**

If you have gone through the discovery phase of the sales cycle and are confident that the customer understands that your product or service addresses his needs, then ask for the sale by asking for an objection: *"Is there any reason why we can't proceed with the shipment?"* This approach allows the customer to raise any final objections if he has any without saying "no" to the sale.

Another example: *"Is there any reason that you wouldn't do business with our company?"* The customer says *"no"* and you say *"Great! Sign on the bottom line."*

Something for nothing

> **"If you sign the order today, I will throw in X at no extra charge."**

A free add-on may be a small and inexpensive gimmick but it can work if handled correctly. *"I happen to have an extra toner with me. If you sign off on the order today, I'll throw it in at no charge."*

Often, an extra bonus seems to make a deal better and it might just be enough to tip the scale in favor of the buying decision. This works well for people who are on the fence.

Impending event

> **"The installation crew will be in your area next week.**
> **When can we schedule an appointment?"**

If you truly have a deadline or reason for the customer to make a quick decision, the impending event closing works well. *"I have an installation crew in town next week. Can we schedule a day with you?"*. If the deadline is in your interest and not the customer's, it will be seen as self-serving and will not work. You can also say: *"I happen to be in your area next week and I could come by and pick up the paperwork personally. Which day works best for you?"*

The Columbo close

> *"Oh, one more thing before I leave...*
> *if you like my product, would you take advantage of it?"*

Not only was the TV character Columbo a fantastic police detective, he was also a wonderful sales person. And while few would ever see Columbo as a sales person, his one famous line has lead to more sales closes than most any other line in sales history.

"Just one more thing", Columbo's famous line, opens doors, removes guards and allows you a glimpse into the unprotected mind of your customer.

I also often used the Columbo technique to pre-qualify a customer. After I finished with my telephone conversation and did my initial pitch I say the following things: *"Thank you very much for your time and goodbye. Oh, one more time before I hang up...if you really like what I have to offer, would you be able to invest $50,000 to $100,000 into this deal?"*

You say it as if you almost forgot to mention it. But in reality this question is well placed and intended. It will show you if the customer is a qualified customer who has the potential to invest that kind of money and you will see if he is generally open to go ahead with a deal like that.

The hard close

> *"You must buy this product now! It is the best for you and you need it."*

Hard closing demands a lot of courage and confidence and should only be used when you have nothing to lose.

While people generally love to buy things, most hate being sold to. And when it comes to the hard close, customers are well aware that you are selling them something.

But despite its negative reputation, sometimes the hard close is the best closing technique to use as long as you use it correctly.

> ### *Some people need to be told what to do.*

Often, the older generation is used to a harsher tone. They follow orders and if you have the authority as a person, you can simply tell him to do it.

Obviously, it needs to be in his best interest, too. But some people are a bit stubborn and don't know what is best for them. You can use this dominant technique only with certain people.

The relationship close

> ### *"If you were my brother, I would recommend this product."*

The golden rule of sales states that if a customer likes you, they will find a reason to buy from you. On the other hand if a customer does not like you, they will find a reason not to buy from you.

Building a relationship with a customer is a sure way to not only close a sale but to create a long-term customer. Unless what you sell is a "one and done" type of product or service, learning how to build rapport with your customers is the most powerful closing tool you will ever enjoy using. Sometimes people buy a product from you even if they don't necessarily need it because they want to do you a favor and because they like you so much.

The take away close

> *"Sorry Mr. Client but I cannot sell this product to you.*
> *It is only for a special group of customers."*

We hate when things are taken away from us. Go and try to take a piece of candy away from a baby and you'll get a very loud example of one simple fact: No one likes having things taken from them. Whether it is something you own or something that you want to own.

But taking things away from your prospects can actually be used as a closing technique.

As with all closing techniques, the take away close takes a discipline professional to know how and when to use it correctly. If used too often or too early, you'll end up negatively affecting your margin. Like every other sale, the Take Away Close is not the "end all, be all" close. Learn it and, more importantly, learn when to use it.

Sometimes you could also make the customer "hot" for an expensive product and then say: *"Why don't you consider the cheaper alternative instead. You probably can't afford this one anyway."*

What happens is that when your customer senses that you are not going to sell them what they want, they often get more aggressive in their pursuit. Never use the take away close as your first means of closing a sale.

After the "no" close

> *"Honestly, what was the real reason why you didn't buy from me?"*

You can still get a sale even after the client said "no" after your presentation.

You are about to leave the client's office, put your hand on the door and then say: *"Mr. Client, I know you didn't want to buy the product from me today. In order for me to improve my presentation skills with other customers in the future, can I please ask you one last question? Since I am about the leave anyway, what was honestly the real reason why you didn't buy from me today?"*

Now, the customer often reveals the real reason, which then will give you a second chance to make the sale.

You say: *"Oh my God, I totally didn't explain to you that our service department will take care of that. Let me quickly explain again..."*

Level with me close

> ## *"Please level with me. Have I failed to show you...?"*

As you approach the end of the selling process and the customer says he wants to think about it, ask him to get to the point: *"Level with me. Have I failed to show you the value that you will receive from your investment?"*

Then be quiet.

You take on the blame by saying that you are sorry for not explaining the product properly. You can also say: *"Mr. Client, can we please be totally honest here for a moment? What did I not explain properly? Why are you so hesitant right now? Let's please just be very honest right now for a moment."*

The balance sheet close

Make a list with the pros and cons

Ben Franklin, the first US diplomat, is said to have made decisions by creating a list with two columns: the pros and the cons.

When he was facing an important decision, he would make two columns and the longer column would be the one that he would choose.

This approach works well with analytical personalities. If you use it as a closing technique, just be sure you have a lot of benefits in the customer's "pro" column.

The fly-fish close

"You will only get a discount if you act now"

You promise something valuable then take it away if a decision isn't made now.

Example: *"We have a special offer for a 20% discount but only if you decide to buy now."*

This is an obvious sales technique that doesn't always work with smart people. But some people only focus on what they would lose if they didn't act that it becomes a big motivation not to lose the discount.

General sales closing tips

> *When you're trying to sell something, the worst thing you can do is sound like you are trying to sell something.*

Unfortunately, people new to selling (perhaps because you've been building a new business) often try to execute simplistic sales techniques that buyers can spot a mile away.

Customers hate it when sellers hammer away at them, trying to close a deal. Nothing creates resistance faster than the old hard sell.

If people feel tricked or otherwise betrayed, they will not only not buy from you now, they may well never buy from you ever again or even turn all their friends against you. In particular beware of using unsubtle techniques with professional buyers, who can usually see them coming from miles away.

There are many closing techniques and there are some common tips that are offered to make closing even more successful.

ABC – Always be closing

ABC is a common term which stands for 'Always Be Closing', which is both good and bad advice.

ABC is good advice when it is used to keep in mind that you are always aiming towards a close. It is bad when you just use it to mean battering the customer to death with a barrage of unsubtle closing techniques.

Silence after

When you have used a closing technique, make sure to be quiet afterwards and let them respond. If you just keep talking, then you may miss what they have to say - like 'yes' for example. Silence also builds tension and will encourage them to respond - and a response to a well-put closing question will hopefully be positive.

Watch emotions

Watch out for the other person not only in what they say but also in the emotions behind the words. Never try closing when they are in a negative emotional state - you will only cause further objection and possibly anger that means they will never buy from you again.

Over-closing

It is not unknown for sales people to talk their customers into closure then carry right on and talk them out again. You can over-do closing and it requires a close sensitivity to avoid this trap.

There is no: "I will be back later"

When a customer says 'I'll be back', sales people in many different situations know that this is just an excuse to leave.

The consequence of this is that when customers say they will be back, you cannot count on it and should treat this as if they will not and decide either to move to the next customer or redouble your sales efforts.

Signals to spot

Signals you can see may be verbal, non-verbal (body language) or specific actions.

1. Verbal signals: things people may say when they are ready to close

- Saying yes or making significant positive noises:
When they are feeling positive about the product, they will also be more generally positive.

- Saying things like 'right' and other decision indicators:
The decision to buy will leak into their language in all kinds of ways.

- Talking about money:
Seeking the best price.

- Asking usage questions:
As they imagine themselves using it and pause at uncertainty points.

- Asking about timescales:
They want is as soon as possible so are interested in delivery, setup, learning, etc.

2. Body language signals: signals that customers may display when they are ready to close

- Showing positivity:
Smiling, nodding and other signs of feeling keen.

- Moving forward:
Including leaning in or even touching you as they seek to connect with you in a more influential way.

- Hurrying:
Talking faster to get to ownership sooner.

- Gazing at or touching the product:
Covetously imagining ownership.

3. Action signals: things that customers may do when they are ready to close

- Reading literature detail:
Repeated examination of information and pictures.

- Taking measurements:
Checking it will fit.

- Playing with the product:
Practicing owning it.

- Bringing others to view it:
Seeking confirmation.

4. Buying signals

When buyers are ready to buy, they will tell you, but not with words. They will, however, send loud non-verbal signals. All you need to do is be able to read them.

5. Customer signals

When customers come into your sights, whether it is a retail store, at an exhibition or in any other environment, they will be sending you signals. The signals that they send will include:

"I am just wandering around with no real interest in products and intention to buy."
"I am interested in this product, but am not currently anxious to buy."
"I am very interested in this and might well buy it if you can answer a few questions."
"I want to buy this, now!"

When they are not ready to buy

When a customer is not ready to buy, it does not mean that they will not buy, but it does mean that you will need a different approach.

Do remember also that if there are many customers around, spending a lot of effort selling to one customer may mean that you miss out on a lot of other easier sales.

1. Avoiding eye contact with you

When you look at them and they immediately look away, they probably do not need assistance right at this moment. Do watch what they are doing, because they may need some help soon.

If they are handling a limited range of products, spending time looking at things, then it may be a good idea to stand nearby, relaxed and ready to help (not anxious and ready to pounce).

When they look at you with a longer glance, move toward them. If they keep looking, keep moving in and start the sale.

2. Making "not now" excuses

If they say 'just looking' or otherwise indicate that they don't need help, then make an encouraging remark to keep them looking and back off. Still keep an eye on them to see if their demeanor changes.

3. Casual handling of the product

If they are casually picking up different products and dropping them back, perhaps not tidily, it can be a big nuisance for you as you tidy up after them (when they have left) but this may well be a symbol of a bored browser.

As ever, keep an eye on them so you can move in when they change how they are behaving.

4. Looking at many different products

If they are wandering around looking at almost random products, spending a similar short time on each one, then they may again be a relatively bored browser.

5. Moving around quickly

When they are moving quite quickly around the place, they may be scanning for something or may be wandering.

If they slow down, watch more carefully and move in when they are showing more signs of interest.

When they are ready to buy

When the person is ready to buy, or at least they are showing some interest, then you should also be ready to pick them up and move them towards the final close.

1. Spending time looking at one product type

When they are looking at one type of product, and especially if you have a broad range from which they are browsing only a small category, then they may well be interested in buying. Perhaps they need advice, so ask if you can help them decide.

> *The longer a person looks at one product type, the more likely they are to buy it. They are investing their time, which is a sure sign of interest.*

2. Looking around for somebody to help them

If you see them looking around, catch their gaze, and perhaps raise your eyebrows a little to signal that you are ready to help. If they sustain the glance or raise their eyebrows too, move in to sell. This is particularly significant if they are holding the product or have just spend time looking at a limited product range.

3. Asking questions about the detail

If, when you offer help, they get into more detail about the product, then they are likely to be becoming more interested.

If they ask about the functionality of the product, they may well have a checklist of things they are seeking, so ask for details of what they are seeking. You can also ask more about how they will use the product, from which you can advice on the best buy for them.

4. Asking about price

This is a good buying signal. You can tell them the price or you can ask how much they are looking to spend today. If they tell you, then you can help them find the best value for the money they have to spend.

5. Using possession language

When they pick up the product, they are getting a sense of owning it. This continues when they talk about how they will use the product -- which is a good reason for encourage this talk.

Look for 'I' language. Get them to use it. Ask how they will use it. You can even talk about it as if they already own it, although be careful of being unsubtle and pushy.

6. Asking another person's opinion

When they ask another person what they think about the product, they are likely thinking about buying the product and are seeking confirmation.

You might thus find yourself selling it to the second person also. Think about this when you are making the initial sale -- include whoever else is there in the sales talking, though do watch for whether the main seller wants to be the main focus or appreciates others being included.

Body state changes

Any transition in non-verbal communication will typically signal a change in mental state that may well indicate readiness to buy. If they suddenly relax after asking questions or discussing the product, this may well signal that they have changed mental state. Other signals include changes in body position, gesture, skin tone, style of talk and so on.

- **Touching the money**

If they touch their wallet or purse and especially if they get out cash or credit card, this is a very strong signal for you. Get to them and ask if you can help. If they say they want to buy, just take their money (and do beware of 'un-selling' the product by your over-zealous and non-needed sales chatter).

Dealing with objections

- **Situation 1:**

Client: *"I have to think about it."*

Sales Person: *"What exactly do you have to think about? Which one specific point is not clear to you?"*

- **Situation 2:**

Client: *"I have to think about it."*

Sales Person: *"That is a great idea. This is an important decision. Obviously, you have a very good reason why you want to think about it. May I ask what that reason is? Is it the price?"*

Keep asking until you have the real reason.

Keep asking control question and eliminate all factor until you have the truth. Sometimes it requires courage to ask for the real reason. But you need to be aware that there should not be anything that he needs to think about.

• **Situation 3:**

Client: *"I have to think about it."*

Sales Person: *"Mr. Client, let's be honest for one moment. What is the real reason why you must think about it?"*

• **Situation 4:**

Client: *"I have to think about it."*

Sales Person: *"How long do you need to think about it?*

Client: *"2 weeks!"*

Sales Person: *"2 weeks? Really? May I ask you a question? How much time will you dedicate to think about the product? 2 hours per day? And this for 14 days? So a total of 28 hours?"*

Client: *"Of course not."*

Sales Person: *"I thought so. I guess you will need an hour the most, right? Yes. So why don't you give me a call tomorrow and let me know?"*

Dealing with two people at the same time (husband and wife)

When you are dealing with two people who are sitting at the same table, you must find out who of the two the real decision maker is.

Sometimes you can convince one person and you think you are close to the end but then you find out that it is the other person who is the real decision maker.

The worst situation is when you have one person and after the whole presentation he says that he needs to ask his wife or husband. Therefore you should always have both present before you make your presentation. Otherwise refuse to start.

Closing different types of people – red, blue, green and yellow type

If you are dealing with the red type, you don't need to go too much into detail and you can have a more dynamic and bold presentation. Your closing can also be something like: *"Do you want to make more money or not? If yes, then sign here!"*

When dealing with the blue type you need to be different. You need to give him rational reasons and data that will support the decision. Also, you will have to go through the fine print of the contract before he will decide to buy. Support your statements with statistics and facts.

When dealing with the green type you must have a great conversation, laugh a lot and tell stories. This type is focused on the relationship and if he likes you, he will do the deal because he thinks that you are a nice person. The product is secondary.

The yellow type wants something special that not everyone has. Therefore, make the product special and use lots of praise and recognition when dealing with this type.

> *When it comes to closing a deal, it is important that you can recognize what kind of person you are dealing with.*

If you keep it general, you won't get very far with the blue type. But if you go into too much detail, you will bore the red type to death. If you are arrogant and don't focus on the person, you will have no chance with the green type.

Closing means that you develop a good relationship with your client based on his personality type and then use the things that he needs to hear to close the sale.

CHAPTER 9

MENTAL LAWS *FOR SALES PEOPLE*

Never cold call again

Cold calling is a waste of time. It is no longer effective.

Imagine that you want to buy a new laptop computer. How do you go about getting one? Do you wait for a person to cold call you?

Of course not! You go on the Internet and you look for the one you want.

You compare different models and then you either order it online or you go to the electronics store and buy the model that you have selected. The sales person there doesn't have to "sell" you the computer anymore. All he has to do is to take the order and you will pay for it.

So why do you think you need to do a thousand cold calls in order to sell anything?

The way that people buy products has changed.
The job of a sales person is order taker and no longer product seller.

Cold calling is no longer effective. Most people are fed up with too many sales calls and too much damage has been done over the last 20 years. People hate to be bothered and technology has made it easy to see who is calling (caller ID) so they won't even answer the phone anymore.

Old school sales people still believe that cold calling is effective but they are wrong.

Cold calling is dead and it is a waste of time, energy and motivation.

Sales and marketing strategies have changed – your attitude must change, too

> *Times have changed.*
> *Things that worked 5 years ago are no longer effective today.*

The days of the aggressive sales person are long gone and while there are still a few old school sales people out there, there has been an evolution of the type of attitude that is needed for a successful sales person. Today's highly successful sales people are the masters of relationship building and understand that subtlety and listening are the keys towards making a sale.

Relationship building has never been more important in the sales process. You need a sales person who understands that they need to listen to their prospects, ask them about their needs and come up with solutions that meet those needs. They also need to be willing to nurture their leads, even if they get a no the first time.

> *The way that people make buying decisions has changed.*

Positioning yourself as an expert and specialist

You are a professional with power and not a beggar. The problem with cold calling is that you put yourself down as a businessperson. You are not on the same level with your client if you have to call him and beg for the business.

> *You need to be seen as a business equal or professional,*
> *not as a sales person.*

People don't really like sales people. They fear that they will be talked into a product that they don't really need or want. People prefer professionals, though. If you need to get your taxes done, you don't want to be cold called by an accountant. That would almost appear shady. You would look for a professional in the phone book or online and then try to get an appointment.

Once you are there, the tax professional is helping you and you are glad to be there. You don't feel like he is trying to sell you his services (even though he is).

> **The way you see yourself determines how others see you.**

Therefore, if you have any kind of product or service to sell, you need to be positioned as a professional and at least as a business equal. People need to be glad to see you. They need your advice as if they went to see a doctor or a lawyer.

> **You cannot solicit clients like a regular sales person.**
> **You need to find a new strategy.**

New ways to find clients

In order to find new clients, you need to find new ways instead of cold calling. Whether you see your clients in person or you sell something online, you still need to incorporate new ways to bring the right people your way. Here are some new ideas:

Google Ads:

Instead of calling people and solicit their business, have them contact you. Place an ad with Google Ads and provide information online about your product. Make it easy for people to request more information and follow up with a newsletter or by phone.

- **Personal referrals:**

There is nothing more powerful and easy than to use personal referrals from existing clients. For six years I never had to make one single cold call. I only used referrals. Develop a system so that you will always get new names and never run out.

- **Newsletters:**

You should use an automated system like Aweber, iContact or Infusionsoft to send valuable information to your list of subscribers.

By doing this on a regular basis, you will eventually get new business. Using an email newsletter is just one way and should be an addition to several other ways.

- **Blog:**

People love blogs. You can go to blogger.com and write about a "problem" that people are interested in. Offer them a solution by redirecting them to your website.

- **Someone else calls first:**

You should never do cold calls yourself because it will destroy your image as a business professional. But you could hire a student or a housewife for $10 per hour to do marketing cold calls for you. This person has to call 100 people in 5 hours and find about 5 qualified leads that are interested in receiving some general information about your product.

Once you have those people who are generally interested (leads), you can follow up with a call. This way your time spent is much more effective and your chances of success increase quite a bit.

- **Flyer with return fax option:**

You can also go from business to business office and hand out flyers. People can request some general information by faxing you back that form. Because it is something tangible people will actually use it and the success quote is much higher than cold calling.

Don't sell anything when you are there. Simply introduce yourself and ask the secretary to give this form to the person making the decision.

Developing a new business idea

Find a problem that is PAINFUL AND URGENT.

In order to sell anything you must have a great marketing message. This message must be a solution to a problem that is painful and urgent. If the product or the message is "nice to have" but not "an absolute MUST", then there is no need for a customer to act.

It all comes down to identifying problems that are painful and urgent. The message "Prevent a virus attack on your computer" is nice and someone might do it someday but it is not a MUST. Things like "Never cold call again" or "Stop my divorce" are messages like that for example. If the message applies to you because you currently have a problem and you are looking for a quick solution, you become an immediate buyer of the product.

In order for someone to act NOW or TODAY the initial step to get more information about the product must be free and with no risk. You can focus on one main problem and the client can download a free report (PDF) to read more about the problem.

Once he has first received some value for free, he is willing to explore what you have to offer further. Because he received your free report, he had to opt-in in your newsletter. Now you have the permission to send him more emails and send him your product offer. So ask yourself again: What problem am I solving for people that is urgent and painful? This is the million-dollar question...

TRUST is more important than ever

People don't believe anything anymore that is written on the Internet.

The main problem today with the growth of the Internet and its sales offers is lack of trust. Where there is an opportunity to make money, there are also the scammers or the people who over-promise and under-deliver (very typical for American sales people).

Since I originally come from Europe where the attitude is more like under-promise and understatement, it can be frustrating to get disappointed when things get over-promised and then the result is mediocre.

People don't trust the marketers anymore – especially on the Internet. Because trust is such a crucial factor these days, you need to refrain from presenting your products in a way that appears to be too sales oriented. If you write your emails and marketing messages like you were writing to a personal friend and in a "normal" manner, your response will be much greater.

> ***Don't try to "sell" anything but rather give people value and show them that you are a normal person that they can trust.***

In order to get clients you need to earn their trust and give them something of value in advance.

Personalized video message instead of "just text"

> ***Personalized video messages are much more effective and trustworthy than simple text.***

Another important finding is that more and more people in the industry are using videos to promote and explain their products.

Videos are not just more interactive and easier for people to understand than plain text but they also show that there is a real person behind the product. A regular person who is the owner of the business is much more real and convincing than a professional actor.

Most people prefer a quick video (max. 5 minutes) to long texts. Both are necessary but you can see more and more Internet gurus promoting their products with a short video message. It is much more effective and trustworthy.

Incorporate as much video message as possible. Most people are more likely to watch a short video than to read a long sales letter.

Make the first contact risk-free

People don't want to sign up for your newsletter and then get spammed with too many emails. Therefore, write the following text when someone is considering to sign up for your newsletter:

"ABC knows that you care how information about you is used and shared, and we appreciate your trust that we will do so carefully and sensibly. We will not share your information with anyone and we will not send you unnecessary emails."

> **You need to make it really easy and risk-free
> for someone to start with the first product.**

Frank Rumbauskas who created the program "Never Cold Call Again" will send you a free 37-page PDF initially. After, he will offer you his program for 30 days for free.

All you have to pay is the $5 shipping free. If you like the program, your credit card will be charged $97 after 30 days. If you don't like it, you can send back the program and you won't get charged. No gimmicks, no follow-up fees, no subscriptions.

This way it is really tempting to buy the product and test it for free. Obviously, most people forget to cancel or send it back because they are lazy. But in reality, the product has some great value and information and because of that, you will keep it.

Do you want to be rich or famous?

When you get into real estate, they tell you to "get your name out there". People think that they need to do a lot of promotion for themselves and so that people know their name. But in reality "getting your name out there" doesn't not lead to more business. Yes, maybe people will recognize you more but the cost of becoming a local celebrity to actually getting clients, is in no relation.

We all love to promote ourselves and make us look more important. But you need to ask yourself one important question: *"Do I want to make money or become famous?"* Trying to become famous and building yourself as a brand can take years and takes a lot of money and effort. Building a business that makes money is much easier. So instead of using your money for personal promotion, you should use it to generate new leads.

Let me give you an example: Let's say that you are in room with 500 other people and you were able to get on stage to introduce yourself. Now, everybody knows you. Do you automatically have clients or more business because of that? Or would it be much more effective to get an envelope with the contact information of the 50 people in this room who are actually ready to buy and who are interested in what you have to sell? Of course! Just getting your name out there is not really helping you to make more business.

You want people who are qualified and open for your products. There are people out there who already looking for what you have to offer.

Your job is simply to make sure that they will find you!

Use common sense

> *Use common sense and a logical*
> *psychological approach when developinga sales process.*
> *Old ways and wishful thinking will lead to failure.*

Use your head and stop daydreaming. Change your approach. Times have changed and what used to work 5, 10 or 20 years ago is no longer effective. People are still the same and they have emotions. But the way you get clients is different. Let me give you the "cookie example":

Let's assume that you come to my house for a visit. I tell you that you can help yourself and go to the fridge and take some cookies out of there. Most likely, you wouldn't do it because you would feel awkward or rude.

That is exactly how a lot of people treat their clients when it comes to marketing. But if you were sitting in the living room and I brought you a plate with cookies and I offered them to you, you would probably take one even if they weren't your favorite cookies. You would almost feel rude to refuse them.

But if I said to you: *"Would you like some cookies? I could go in the kitchen and bake some for you"*; you would probably decline because you don't want me to go out of my way. And again, when it comes to marketing, that same rule applies.

If I offered you something like for example a subscription for a newsletter, you would accept it. But if I said that I could go out of my way for you, you wouldn't go for it. So when it comes to marketing you should use common sense.

Don't expect people to come to you or to do something that is out of the ordinary. But if you offer them something where it is easy for them to say "yes", they are more likely to accept what you have to offer.

Internet marketing

> *Give the people what they want – not what you think they should have*

The cool thing with Google Adwords is that you can see what people are looking for on the Internet. There are ways to find out what the most popular searches are and you can see how many people were looking for a particular phrase that day.

Frank Kern, an Internet marketing guru who made $18 million in 24 hours on the Internet started exactly this way. He was looking for the most popular searches and he found that 80,000 people were looking for "How to get your parrot to talk".

He knew nothing about parrots whatsoever but then he went on Elance.com and hired a vet who specialized in parrots to write a book about that topic. It cost him about $600 to have that book written but he sold the program for thousands of dollars. He simply gave the market and the people what they were looking for.

John Reese who made $1 million on the Internet in one day says that you simply need to test your online strategy and if you can proof your concept by simply making $1, then you know your strategy is basically working. All you have to do after is to tweak and improve it.

He says that Internet marketing is basically like running a lemonade stand. You invest $3 for the lemonade in the beginning, sell one cup for $1, sell 10 cups and your profit is $7.

You also need to invest into marketing and ads on the Internet but in today's day and age it is at a fraction of the cost compared to what it used to be. The leverage and the amount of people that you can reach are unbelievable.

> *Testing, eliminating and improving*
> *will lead to success – one small step at a time.*

If something doesn't work because it was the wrong strategy, you will know immediately.

In the old days it might have cost you thousands of dollars and you had to wait months to see if you ad was giving you any return.

Developing a business based on your ideal lifestyle and not on the business needs

What is the purpose of your work? To have a better life!

Dean Jackson who made millions online teaching Real Estate agents how to be more effective, said that he rather wants to enjoy a great lifestyle, even though he could make more money.

He came up with a list of different things on what that really meant for him. The quality of your life is dependent on how you happy you are. Work is a big part of it. Here is his list:

1. Work your own hours and be able to work from anywhere in the world
2. You don't have to wear a suit
3. Your passive income exceeds your current cost of living
4. You work only on projects that you are excited about
5. You don't deal with whinny people (complain or are difficult)
6. Get up in the morning whenever you want
7. Follow your hobbies and passions
8. Have more time available for the family and the kids
9. You don't need to take on every opportunity that comes your way
10. You are not bound to a local business

What is your definition of success? When is it enough? How much money do you really need?

> **You don't need $100 million to be happy and enjoy the lifestyle that you want. You can organize your life in such a way that you can enjoy a great lifestyle and still make enough money.**

With today's technology it is possible to live anywhere you want, work from home and the Internet has thousands of opportunities for you to make money.

There has never been a better time to enjoy a great life/work balance. But you need to decide for yourself what you really want and what is important to you.

Setting goals and clarity

> **Someday leads to a town called nowhere.**

"Someday I will buy myself a mansion. Someday I will get my dream car. Someday I will be successful – you will see!"

There is Monday, Tuesday, Wednesday, Thursday, Friday, Saturday and Sunday. But Someday doesn't exist.

> **Clarity is one of the most important things for success.**

In order to be successful at anything it is important to have absolute clarity about your goals. You need to define your goals as detailed as possible.

Change your approach – use leverage

> ## No one is really smarter or better than you.
> ## They are simply using a smarter or better strategy.

The Internet offers new opportunities how business is done. For a fraction of the cost compared to traditional advertising you can place an ad for pennies or a few dollars and get results.

The time and investment is nothing compared to what it used to be in order to get clients. You need to become a specialist on using the Internet and its marketing tools.

You need to use leverage. Be smart about your approach. If you don't try it you will never know if it works. Also, ten or twenty years ago, infomercials were a very powerful marketing tool. But today, people don't watch infomercials anymore. With the new DVR recording devices, people record their TV shows and skip over the commercials.

Basically, you need to take your infomercial about your company online. Write a report, use videos and make it interactive. You can target a lot more people today than you were able to do in the past.

Whatever you do, you must learn everything about online marketing and test different strategies.

One way to learn about the process is simply to go to other successful companies and see how they sell their products online to you. You can copy their strategies and learn the process.

> ## People are still people – despite all the new technology.

People are still people and they still all have the same wants and needs.

Technology has changed how we can find these people and how we can sell our products. But keep in mind that you still need to use emotions and apply psychological principals to motivate your clients to buy.

You are responsible for your own success

There people in the same industry, in the same market, with the same products, selling to the same clients, making 10 times more than you.

You are the only person who is responsible. It is no one's fault but yours if you succeed or not. There are no excuses and no one is coming to the rescue.

The best sales people are those who display high levels of motivation and hold themselves accountable for their own performance. By referring to sales people I also refer to business people in general since every businessperson is automatically a sales person.

If things don't work out, don't blame anybody but yourself.
You are always responsible for your success.

It doesn't mean that it is easy or that you don't have to deal with obstacles or difficult people but it means that you are ultimately in charge of your own fate.

Wishful thinking is one of the main reasons by people or businesses fail. Only when you take charge of your results and see things as they really are, you can accomplish results.

A negative attitude is the beginning of the end

> **The wrong attitude is like sand in an engine.**
> **First, you need to clean it out before you can get anywhere.**

Being positive is not always easy. I have found that there are basically two kinds of people - those who take responsibility for their lives and those who blame others.

People who take responsibility for their situations are positive people who see the world as a good place. They have made the conscious decision to be this way.

This is not easy; however, understanding these basic principles about attitude are the first steps.

Keep in mind that choosing your mental attitude is the only thing you can control in your life. The most important thing I've learned in my life is that positive thoughts produce positive results and negative thoughts produce negative results.

A positive attitude is more than just "looking on the bright side"; it's a conscious choice to always see the possibilities, the way through and the way out of even the worst of circumstances.

Do people who are successful and happy have a positive attitude because they are successful and happy? Or are they successful and happy because they have a positive attitude?

I've never met anyone I would consider happy or successful at anything that had a negative attitude.

> **There are only two kinds of people in the world: Those who**
> **think they can and those who think they can't. They are both right.**

Self-confidence is key

Believe in yourself even when no one else does.

An effective sales person displays healthy levels of self-confidence – not arrogance. You need to be able to tell the difference between the two traits. An arrogant attitude is not a trait you want in a sales person in today's marketplace. Self-confident candidates will be modest, while still talking about their achievements and their personal goals.

People will not follow people who show doubt. In order to succeed as a sales or a businessperson you must have a healthy level of self-confidence. You must believe in your company and your products and you must demonstrate that you are one of the best in your field. I have seen many sales people who were unsure about their products and because of that the customers could feel that something was not 100% right. In the end, those sales people failed because their energy that they gave off made it impossible to convince anyone.

Self-confidence has to do with happy, positive energy and the conviction of what you have to offer. Psychologists tell us that one of the best ways to build our self-image and improve our attitude is to keep the commitments we make to ourselves.

As a result, we will gain confidence, improve our outlook and build on those successes.

Nelson Mandela, after being freed from 27 years of imprisonment in South Africa, was interviewed by reporters who asked him how it felt to finally be a free man. *"I have always been a free man"* he said. *"I always knew that someday I would once again feel the grass under my feet and walk in the sunshine."*

Attitude is more than simply reacting to a situation or circumstance in a positive way. It is about understanding the reality of a situation and choosing to see the possibilities in it, regardless. A consistently positive attitude transcends the reality of "what is" and becomes, instead, "what can be."

When it comes to selling, your attitude and enthusiasm make all the difference. Combine the two and, with good education and well-developed skills, you will have the foundation on which to build a successful sales career.

Protect your own energy

> *"Getting knocked down in life is a given.*
> *Getting up and moving forward is a choice."*
> (Zig Ziglar)

No one is always successful. That is not normal – no matter what others make you believe. There are always good times and bad times. It is the circle of life.

The key to getting through difficult times is to realize that those bad times won't last forever. They will pass and better times always follow. As a sales person you need to be in a good, happy and energetic mood if you are dealing with customers. Unfortunately, that is not always possible. When things are difficult you need to stay positive as good as you can believe that times will be better again. You need to protect your own positive energy.

Sometimes it is better to avoid certain situations or people because they can negatively influence your energy. You don't need to be confronted with problems all the time. You need to protect yourself from problem and plan your life accordingly.

If there are people in your life who suck the positive energy out of you, you need to avoid them or get rid of them. Without your positive energy, you will not be able to perform well.

Keep your energy level high at all times. Go to the gym every day. Physical fitness leads to mental fitness. You can deal much better with stressful situations if you are doing physically well. Exercise also helps you to reduce stress and keeps you more balanced.

It is all your head — success or failure

Most people need a crisis to finally make changes in their lives.

If you are in a place where things are not too bad and they are not great either, you will not make drastic changes. This is called the comfort zone. Most people stay in a state where they get by but they are not really moving forward, either.

Sometimes a crisis or hitting rock bottom is what you need to make the changes necessary to improve your life. A negative event appears to be negative in the beginning but sometimes it can be the best thing that happens to you. My brother in law had to go to prison for one year. He said that his life was going downhill at the time and that he was losing himself. Going to prison helped him to find himself again and his life is much better now. It was initially hard but in the end it was exactly what he had needed.

Success is always a mental game. It is not based on luck or chance.

My friend Oskar who is a great sales person had a few months where nothing seemed to work out at all. He couldn't close any deals anymore. The more he thought about it, the more negative he became. He was almost ready to quit.

When I talked to him I tried to remind him that success is only in his head. I told him that no matter how bad his situation was; the only way to change it is to change your mental attitude.

That is actually one of the biggest secrets of millionaires. It is not skill, ability or knowledge that makes you successful but a strong and powerful mindset.

When I became a millionaire it was the main reason why I made so much money. It was all in my head and my mental attitude to achieve success was very focused and strong.

At the time, an old friend who I hadn't seen in years saw how financially successful I had become. He said to me: *"Wow, you were really lucky!"* My reply: *"Luck has nothing to do with it. It is all just a mental game!"*

Don't sabotage yourself

> *Alcohol, drugs, pills, food and excessive spending*
> *are covering up a pain and you are sabotaging yourself.*

Maybe this point doesn't apply to you but there are a lot of sales people out there who self-sabotage themselves. They use drugs, alcohol or gamble to cover up some pain. Some people make a lot of money but then they also spend everything. I have seen brilliant people destroy themselves by living a lifestyle that was excessive and unhealthy. They made millions of dollars during their best times but then just a few years later they were broke and mentally incapable of getting back on top.

Pain needs to be uncovered. If you are trying to cover up some pain, then deep down you feel like you don't deserve success. You can't continue to numb yourself and expect to be happy.

Sometimes talking to a therapist or a person who has nothing to do with your family or work can help you to see things in a different light.

You need to go for it despite fear and doubt

> *There are more opportunities available than ever before. We live*
> *in the best time ever. But the way people buy products has changed.*

You can have, do or be anything. You have all the options available. Most people hold themselves back because of fear. They have fear of rejection and fear of failure. But the only way to move forward is to face your fears and then they will disappear.

> *Laziness, doubt and inactivity kill more dreams than failure.*

Your energy will go to where your focus is. That is where results happen. People who are afraid are also paralyzed. They don't take action because they worry too much and have doubt in their own abilities. But it is not our actions that create negative results. It is not taking action. If you take action, there will always be a result. The worst is laziness, doubt and fear. It will destroy your self-confidence and your life.

Everything can change in an instant

> *The keys to success are a single piece of information, a single idea at the right time, in the right situation that can change your life.*

The main reason why I write these programs is to encourage others. I know that most people read books of successful authors and many things that I write about are not new pieces of information.

But what I am hoping is that you will get one insight, one single piece of information that will change your business life for the better. One idea or strategy can change everything.

Sometimes we are doing everything right but the results are not satisfactory. By changing one thing or getting one piece of advice, things will improve. Therefore, I urge you to read all my materials. I hope it will help you to improve your life.

CHAPTER 10

20 YEARS
SALES
EXPERIENCE

Welcome — there are no limits

I have decided to write about the last 20 years of my sales career. I wanted to describe the ups and the downs of that time and encourage other people to choose the profession of the sales person.

This text is dedicated to the people who...
1. Have chosen the path of the sales person and are at the beginning of their career.
2. Still have to find out that selling is the basis for any big success in life.
3. Realize that selling will turn them into a mentally stronger and happier person.

The insights and lessons that I will describe are real and from actual experience.

Why am I qualified to talk about sales? Here is a quick look at my story:
At the age of 20 I got into straight commission sales in a financial planning sales organization. At the age of 21 I was earning $10,000 a month.

By the time I was 23, I became the number one sales team leader in our company in Europe. There were 1000 other team leaders that I had to compete against. By that time I had hired and trained over 75 sales people. In the six years I was with this financial planning company I have had over 3000 face-to-face meetings with clients.

Eventually, I got so good at my job that I had a perfect closing rate for over nine months. Usually, my closing rate was somewhere between 80 and 90%. During that time my team and I had raised over $400 million in financial and insurance products.

I taught other sales people how to become better in sales. I taught them topics like sales techniques, communication, financial consulting and financial basics.

When I went into the hedge fund industry I became the global sales manager for the biggest independent hedge fund company in the world. I managed a team of very bright and sometimes-arrogant young people with impressive University degrees and we improved the overall sales team result from $42 million in a four month period to over $245 million just one year later.

We raised the money from financial professionals, banks and institutional clients.

During my entire career I hired, fired, motivated, encouraged, trained, led, promoted, evaluated and educated a lot of new sales people and employees.

I built my own companies and raised millions for them though Private Equity. I had several sales organizations and over 60 people working for me.

At the age of 30, I decided to start my own business and only two and a half years later, I became a millionaire. I had raised over $40 million for my companies and projects.

I had founded, managed and owned 11 US companies, 5 Swiss companies, one Canadian company and several offshore companies. I had built three sales teams and over 60 people in six different countries were working for me. I was earning over $100,000 per month.

All this sounds like a great career but I had a hard time when I started and in between I also had times when I was completely burnt out from selling and didn't want to see any clients at all.

In my opinion, you can't run from your destiny and once you have decided to embrace the topic of selling wholeheartedly your life will change for the better.

> *Every business transaction has to do with selling*
> *and whether you like it or not you should try*
> *to learn everything there is to know about this topic.*

Handing down knowledge to my son – the natural sales talent

When my son was five years old we had the following conversation:

Jackson: *Daddy, do you love me?*

Norman: *Of course, I love you!*

Jackson: *If you love me, then you only want the best things for me, right?*

Norman: *Of course*

Jackson: *Can you buy me this toy then? Because you love me, right?*

He looked at me with a smile and his bright eyes and it was impossible for me to say "no" in that moment. Every father has a certain type of knowledge that he would like to hand down to his children. Some people are good a building houses, others are musical and are great with cars. The knowledge that I can hand down to my children, has to do with sales and communication.

No matter what anybody does with his or her life knowing the topic of communication will always be a helpful tool. The more you know about it, the more successful you will be – no matter in what industry or area. Selling is the basis for every business transaction and most self-made millionaires are involved in the sales process of their business.

The best sales people in the world are not natural talents who were simply born with these skills. All sales skills were learned and that is good news because everyone can learn these skills.

> *Everybody wants to be successful and make a lot of money.*
> *But it is not intelligence or technical knowledge that make you rich.*
> *It is the ability to sell yourself, your ideas and products.*

If you want to know the secret of making money you should study everything there is to know about sales. It will give you the tools and the understanding in dealing effectively with other people.

Some sales people are so successful that they earn more than one million dollars per year. Luckily, I was one of those people, too. But success in sales or in business is not achieved overnight. It is a process of learning and improving. It is mainly a mental game. But once you have really figured it out there is no limit to what you can achieve.

So the main question is why some sales people are more successful than others. The answer lies in the law of cause and effect. Nothing happens without a reason. There is always a cause (= action) that precedes any kind of result. Success is not an accident. Failure also has reasons.

If you want to know what the difference between success and failure is you need to do what other successful people have done and then do the same.

What others have done before you, you can do as well.

My personal sales story

When I was 20 years old I finished school and was ready to go to the University of Zurich to study Psychology. The reason why I chose Psychology was because I had no real idea what I was going to do with my life. I was good at everything but not outstanding in one thing in particular. I had originally wanted to become a journalist or an actor but there was no burning desire in any of my choices. So in the end I chose to study Psychology because my father was a psychologist.

During the summer before my first semester I spent a lot time at the public outdoor pool. That s where I met David, my sister's ex-boyfriend. He was asking me about my future plans and I told him that I would go on a seven-week trip to America and then I would start with University. He asked me bluntly if I wanted to earn $10,000 per month part-time and still study at the same time.

When I told my girlfriend about the $10,000 she was totally skeptical. She said that this was impossible and that it was a complete pipedream.

During my holidays I kept talking about making $10,000 per month and I started to daydream about it. I had no idea how this would be possible but I believed in it and I think that this was a big part of actually making it happen. So when I finally came back I started my 12 lessons per week at the University and at the same time I started my new job as a financial planner at AWD in Zurich. AWD was the largest independent financial planning company in Europe but it was built like a multi-level marketing company.

When I started to study I was very disappointed with the boring content that was taught at the University. I was reading self-help books and went to seminars but what I learned in class was far away from my interests. I was supposed to study for the next four years and just the thought of that made me feel frustrated.

AWD was a company that offered a financial planning service for clients. We sold a lot of investment and insurance products and earned commissions for the products that we sold. There was no base salary and everything was based on 100% commission. But AWD was also a sales organization where you could become team leader or sales manager and where you would hire new employees to build your team. And of course you would also get a percentage of everything that your own people sold.

The things that I learned during my time at AWD were invaluable for my life. I learned how to sell, how to communicate, how to present and how to lead employees.

> *It was not only an education from a business point of view but also important lessons for life and for dealing with personal relationships.*

Working in a sales organization was a lot of fun. We were a lot of like-minded people who were money hungry and there was a constant competition between us. Most of my peers were in their early twenties and we were making a lot of money. Everyone drove an expensive car and we were all dressed in brand name suits. I have a lot of positive memories from that time and I was learning so much for my own life. I had no fixed schedule and was free to work whenever I wanted. But I worked a lot and did my best to move up in my career.

I believe that the freedom of being able to make your own schedule is great and I could never work in a different way after that. No one told me when I had to show up for work and the quality of that lifestyle was great. But with freedom comes responsibility. You cannot constantly take time off and expect to make money. So that is why I had a lot of personal goals that drove me to perform at a high level.

At the same time I was learning everything about sales, rhetoric, communication and applied psychology with actual clients while I was working at the sales organization. It was so much more interesting than University and I felt that I finally found my destiny.

After two and a half months of University I simply couldn't take it anymore. I felt so unhappy but I was afraid what people would say if I quit. But when it came to my new sales job, I was also not very successful. I was really scared of cold calling. Basically, I was afraid of rejection.

At this point I felt like a prisoner of my own choices. I didn't want to go back to University and I didn't want to do any more cold calls. I felt like the only choice that I had left was to go back to the grocery store where I worked part-time as a student.

> **When you first start out in sales you will experience failure.**
> **That is unavoidable. The trick is not to give up**
> **and learn from it despite the pain it causes.**

Luckily, my sales manager recognized that I needed help. He scheduled an hour with me to make phone calls. He sat next to me and forced me to call everyone on my list. With his help, I was able to set several appointments and I can honestly say that it was a turning point in my sales career. It broke the ice and from that point on I was able to do the calls by myself.

I realized that all of my fears were unfounded and after a good conversation with my sales manager I also decided that I didn't want to be an average person making an average salary. I decided to stand out of the masses and become someone important.

Only six months later I became team leader. At the age of 21 I finally made over $10,000 a month (like I dreamed about). Back then it was a lot of money for a young man.

> *Make peace with prospecting and selling. If you fully embrace it, it will pay you back much more than you can imagine today.*

But I also realized that my real talent was by teaching others to become successful, too.

So I built my sales team and trained more and more sales people as time went on. I even became one of the few who were able to train and educate the entire organization in the topics of sales, communication, financial planning and investments.

At the time I was only 23 years old and many in my audience were more than twice my age. One of my specialties was to get referrals from clients. Except for the beginning I never had to do any more cold calls but solely worked with referrals.

As a financial planner I brought a lot of financial advantages to my clients, which was a good feeling. In my six-year career at AWD I eventually became a team manager and was in the top 20 of the entire organization.

Experiencing a burn out

After six years I got completely burnt out. I simply couldn't deal with any more clients. I was sick to saying the same things over and over again. At the same time I decided to leave Switzerland and start a new life in Vancouver, Canada.

Because I had about $500,000 in stocks I didn't need to work at first. I was newly married and my son was only five months old at the time.

I thought that I had it made and I decided to continue my career in the financial industry but NOT in sales. I went to the Canadian Securities Institute and I enrolled in every single course that they had to offer. In only 9 months I passed several exams and got 12 finance diplomas and designations.

My initial problem in Canada was that no one recognized my European financial education and experience and therefore I thought that if I had the Canadian education that I would easily get a job in a financial firm in Canada.

But I was mistaken.

Unfortunately, it was during the time when the terrorists hit the World Trade Centers in New York on September 11, 2001. After this event, the economy collapsed and most companies didn't want to hire anyone at all. I applied to several jobs and it seemed impossible to get hired because I was competing against hundreds of other applicants.

Here is the funny part: the only jobs that I got offered were sales jobs! I could work as an insurance agent on straight commission or as a stockbroker on a tiny base salary and commission. I really hated these choices. I was trying to avoid getting a sales job but the only jobs that I could get were in sales! I tried to avoid getting a sales job at all cost.

Unfortunately, my stocks fell from $500,000 to $50,000 in value and the 9 months that I didn't work ate up most of my free capital.

In the end I had no choice but to take on the job as a stockbroker. There was a three months training program, which I completed and three months later I gave up because I was still burnt out.

With my tail between my legs and a hurt pride I decided to move back to Switzerland.

Within a week I had 3 job offers and I decided to work for a hedge fund company as a global sales manager leading eight sales people and two admin staff. At the time I was only 28 years old.

When I took over the team, the team result budget for raising capital for institutional clients was $30 million for a four-month period and the result was $42 million. Because of my experience I was able to train the existing sales people and four months later the result went from $42 million to $91 million.

My superiors were happy with the result but they increased my budget from $30 million to $75 million for the next period. Well, I can happily say that my result of $245 million surprised everyone the following period.

Even though I took the sales team from $42 million to $245 million in only one year, I was actually an employee and my income was not going up significantly because of this. I had a good income but I made millions for the company and I felt like I should have been on commission.

The worst part of this position was that I was criticized for my poor administrational skills and my entire review was very negative. I felt very unappreciated and after a year and a half I decided to quit. But because they liked my training so much, I was hired as an independent sales trainer for the sales people and I continued to give seminars and trainings for the staff.

The turning point

Because of my communicational skills I was able to get almost any job if I had an interview.

One day I applied with UBS, the biggest bank in Switzerland. I applied for a job to as a trainer and educator for their staff. They offered me the job for a salary of $150,000 per year. It would have been a job that I would have enjoyed because I like to teach and train others.

But then I did the math. I needed $100,000 per year to live comfortably and I could put away about $50,000 per year. So after 10 years I would have $500,000 in savings. After this quick calculation I decided to decline the job offer and start my own business.

Then there was also something else that happened that changed my life forever. In one week I personally experienced 3 deaths. A person from payroll died, a friend's brother that I just met died and one night I got home and there was a dead cat on the street. I was confronted with death and the meaning of life. Logically, I wondered about the meaning of my own life. I thought if I worked in a regular job working for someone else I would "waste" my talents and my life and it became even more clear to me that I had to go into business for myself.

Selling my own products

When I was a sales person working for big financial companies it was very easy. Those companies had millions of dollars, had a great reputation and I could hide behind the name.

But when I was starting my own company and sold shares to clients, I had to sell myself. It was much harder because there was no one backing me up. I first created a gold company and in the beginning there was not much in the company. So when I sold shares of the company to investors, there was little substance and basically it was just a piece of paper with a dream on it.

At the time I was 30 years old and luckily I was not alone. My partner was Bruno and he was 50 years old and ex-banker of UBS. His main strength was to contact clients and get appointments because he is a very likable person. But when it came to giving the sales presentation, I was better suited and skilled to do it. This way we were an ideal combination.

When we started we got the first two clients in the first month for a total of $16,000 in investments. It was not much but it was a start. But the following month our result was zero!

I was completely devastated and down. I had all this sales experience and talent but I couldn't even create a proper sales result on my own. I almost gave up. I was so negative and frustrated. But it was during this time when it helped to have a partner. Bruno was very happy and optimistic and said that he might have a client for $50,000. His positive attitude and optimism alone helped me to get out of that hole. Eventually, everything turned out well and we raised over $40 million in 2 ½ years.

> **A positive attitude and being optimistic can make all the difference.**

My life changed for the better when I fully and wholeheartedly embraced selling again in my life. It was when I made it my priority and had fun dealing with clients.

It can definitely help to get a break from selling for a while to recharge your batteries. But you should realize that there is no business possible without sales.

General lessons that I learned from being in sales

> **If others have done it before, you can do it, too.**
> **Find out what they have done and then copy their actions.**

I have found that almost anybody can become a sales person. Sales skills are learnable and I have seen average people turn into great sales people.

Becoming a great sales person is not necessarily all about using techniques but doing the things necessary to produce sales. It is important to work on your technique and improve your sales presentation. But it is more important to make many phone calls, see many clients and have the chance to make a sale.

I have seen many very talented people fail because they were lazy. But I have also seen many average people succeed because they were active and not lazy. In the end you need to do the things that other successful people have done and then copy their strategies and actions.

> **Average sales people can compensate their weaknesses**
> **by setting a lot more meetings than others.**

The main problem that new sales people have is the fear of rejection. But even if they can overcome this fear it will be the inexperience of dealing effectively with clients that will hold them back.

Learning from other successful sales people, reading books about sales or going to a sales seminar can definitely help to improve the performance. But in the end nothing beats actual experience. The more meetings with clients someone has, the better he will get because he is exposed to more different situations and people. You can basically become better by seeing more clients and therefore overcome some of your weaknesses in your ability to sell.

But it also has another effect. If you have a full calendar with appointments, you are not so dependent on a single client and the level of your self-confidence will go up. You will not have the attitude of a "beggar" to close a deal and people can feel it. If you are not dependent on closing one particular deal then you have a lot less pressure and you are more likely to close the deal.

You need to identify yourself 100% with the company and the products that you are selling. If you are not in it with your whole heart, you will not succeed.

If you don't believe in your products and in your company then it is very hard to sell. You should educate yourself about every detail and get very excited about it. If you don't have the fire in you, then you cannot expect the spark to get over to your client.

In order to sell you need to be excited yourself. Sometimes all you need is excitement and the rest will take care of itself. No technique or sales presentation can beat excitement.

Learn absolutely everything about your products and industry. Read books and become a real expert in your field.

One of the most important points in becoming a great sales person is to learn absolutely everything about your products and your industry. The more you know, the more competent you will appear.

This is actually a real important point because it is not just the client who can feel that you are an absolute professional in your field but it is also for your own identification with your profession. If you put your whole heart into it, you cannot but succeed.

> *Dream big and constantly set high goals. Even if you only reach 70% of your goals you will be much further ahead.*

They say if you shoot for the moon and you don't get there then you will at least land among the stars. I must say that I find this statement to be true.

When I used to set my sales goals I hardly ever reached them. But because I set them high I would get close and the result was still very good. It is better to set higher goals than realistic and attainable goals because higher goals will motivate you to do more.

> *The only way to really grow and make a lot more money is if you can duplicate yourself and build a sales team.*

If you stay a one-man show there is a limit to the amount of money that you can make. Once you realize that the next step in your development as a sales person is to build a team with other sales people you will be able to increase your income.

It is a logical step to teach others how to sell and to earn a percentage of their sales. When I was a team leader I had 25 sales people under my direct supervision. Because I had so many direct sales people I wasn't able to make any sales personally anymore and I lived fully off the team.

> ### *You need to find the key team leaders that can build a team so that your whole organization can grow.*

The next step is to become a sales manager. But in order to be a successful sales manager you need also great team leaders. Without the right team leaders you cannot maintain a solid organization.

Therefore having the right five key people is the most important thing. Without the right base you cannot grow because you constantly have to help the weak team leaders with their people.

> ### *Hire young and money hungry people.*

There is a saying: *"You can't teach an old dog new tricks."*

If you hire older sales people it can have its advantages. Some of the older sales people can give your team some stability. But honestly I feel that you will do much better and get the sales stars if you mainly hire young and money hungry people. You can influence and motivate younger people much better and they will work harder because they still have a lot to prove.

> ### *Allow yourself to have at least 6 weeks of holidays per year and several extended long weekends away from home to recharge your batteries.*

t is easy to get burned out as a sales person. If you are constantly give it your all and deal with a lot of rejection and "craziness" you will need breaks.

have found that you can make more money as a sales person than if you were simply working n a regular job. Therefore you should also give yourself a reward on a regular basis.

Once you start to plan your year in advance you should also plan at least 6 weeks of holidays and extended weekends to recharge your batteries. Taking time off can compensate the price you pay of working long hours.

> *Plan your week and your personal time in advance*
> *so that you leave nothing to chance.*

When it comes to time management I would suggest that you plan about 70% of all business and personal time in advance. The key to success in sales lies not in achieving one great result once in a while but in the consistency and your overall result.

> *Never be lazy – especially if you have become great in sales. It will not*
> *only kill your income but also your motivation and self-confidence.*

The law of growth says that something that isn't growing must die. This is a law of nature and it also applies to us. If you don't continually try to grow and get better you will eventually fail and become obsolete.

The problem is that we are all creatures of habit and if we take on bad habits, we will get used to them and our performance will go down.

This will have a negative effect on your motivation and your self-confidence. It will take away your joy and all of a sudden work becomes hard and difficult.

My mentor used to say that there are no lazy people. There are only people without real goals.

Think about it. If you are lazy then you are either afraid of rejection and failure or you don't have enough compelling goals that drive you.

> ## *Make a conscious decision to become the best sales person in your company or field.*

This statement seems obvious but in reality it isn't. 85% of people in any field are just doing average. They know enough to get by and they never consciously make the real decision to become one of the best and rise to the top.

Once you actually make that decision, things will never be the same. Everything will change for you. But this decision comes with a price and you need to be aware of it.

The price is that you must work hard and learn absolutely everything there is to know about your field or industry. Also, you must be aware that you must cut back on certain things in your private life that simply won't have any priority anymore.

> ## *Be very smart about your approach. Talk to other sales people and learn something from everyone you talk to.*

You must be spinning your wheel and use an approach to get clients that is very time-consuming or hard. Maybe your strategy is not the best.

You should continually look at the things that you are doing and figure out if there are better and more efficient ways.

I suggest that you go for lunch with other successful sales people and pick their brains. Ask them about their process and you will be astonished how much better you could do.

> ## *Some people are so persistent and annoying that people will eventually say yes just to get the person off their back.*

I have seen sales people with below average intelligence or skill that created great sales results because they were so persistent.

They wanted to succeed so badly that they simply didn't take "no" for an answer from any client. And if they got a "no" then they continued to ask for the sale until the client eventually gave in and said yes.

> ### *The actions of a sales person and his mental attitude are much more relevant than the ones who have a big mouth.*

I have had a sales person who was very impressive and could talk like no other. But he failed miserably. He was all show and there was no action behind his words. And then there was this introverted guy that I was not sure about and he ended up becoming one of the best sales people. His attitude was goal-oriented and because he was coming across as not threatening, people trusted him more.

> ### *Internal motivation is key if you want to succeed in sales.*

Money can be a big motivator but your motivation must be internal. External motivation from your sales manager or from your company is great but if you don't have the inner drive to want to succeed beyond the normal scope, you will always struggle.

Building my first sales organizations

When I was first selling shares of my own company to investors we were only a small organization with a handful of people. Then one day I got a call from a sales person who was actually trying to sell a similar deal to me.

He sent me some marketing material and then a more experienced sales person followed up and called me a week later. This sales person tried to sell me his investment over the phone and I decided to invite him to my office.

He showed up and instead of him selling the investment to me, I sold him on my investment and he decided to take $18,000 from another investor and put it into my deal.

A short time after that he decided to quit his job and joined my organization. He brought with him two more guys and the first month they started to make phone calls to potential investors from a small office in our building. After a month they raised $250,000 and then I decided to get a nice office downtown for them. Within a couple of months we had over 25 sales people in that office and they were all selling my product. It was absolutely amazing.

In the first year that team raised over $10 million from investors. And all was over the phone. It was a little bit like the movie "The Wolf of Wall Street" but obviously legal and not so crazy.

The guy I put in charge of the sales team as the sales manager was called Yves. Yves was an unbelievable sales person. He didn't look like much when you saw him. He was in his late twenties, was very skinny, had yellow teeth, he had a drug and alcohol problem and if you saw him in person you would never in a million years trust him with your money.

But when he was on the phone it was different. His ability to talk to investors was just amazing. He could get someone who decided not to invest to change his mind and 10 minutes later the client would send in the order. He turned every "no" into a "yes".

When he started in my organization he was in debt over $50,000 from a personal loan. In the first year he made over $500,000, spent it all and after that year he was still $50,000 in debt.

It can be fun to work in a sales organization with other like-minded people. There is always action and if you feel down, there is someone who can cheer you up. Money flows and life can be a lot of fun.

Other sales organizations

I also started several other sales organizations. I had several teams in Switzerland but also in some eastern European countries. I started sales teams in America and even bought a licensed brokerage firm and trained new stockbrokers.

Some organizations were doing great while others failed or collapsed. I met hard-core sellers and people who were selling illegally. I have seen it all. One time I invested over $400,000 in one year into one organization. But unfortunately the company failed and I had to close it down.

> **The success of a sales organization depends on the sales manager and the main people involved.**

If you have weak sales people and no sales stars, it is hard for others to see what could be possible. And because of that you create a team of bad performers.

One of the main things in a sales team is the overall mood and motivation. If you have a lot of people who are successful and who are making money, you will breed more of the same. But if you have an organization where people are failing, it is very hard to change the team because no one believes in success. And when people are not making enough money they start to criticize the product or the organization and the overall mood will be very negative.

Once we had a great and talented sales person in our team but he has a negative influence on others. We ended up firing him because his negative attitude was affecting the result of other sales people. Sometimes one person can destroy an entire team. Therefore, you must choose you people well.

> **It all starts with a great sales manager. If you have a strong and almost military-like manager people will do much better.**

At one point I even hired German speaking sales people who were living in America to make marketing sales calls to clients in Europe. Because of the 9-hour time difference some of my sales people started working at midnight. Most started between 4 and 5 am.

This was a system that was working. Sometimes it is better to separate your sales people from the marketing people. The marketing people are simply creating leads and sending out marketing material to clients. But the sales people sit in a different office and sell the products from there.

Losing everything and falling into a hole again

After making millions with my sales organizations and being very successful financially I also experienced times again when I had was out of money and had zero motivation anymore.

Apparently, this happens to a lot of people in my business. You rise to the top, make a lot of money, live like a rock star but then something bad happens. Your deal goes south and you lose all your money and your reputation.

This is exactly what happened to me. My lawyer back then told me that this happens to all successful dealmakers in the stock business and if I can recover from it, I will get out stronger and better in the future.

Well, the time that I was feeling sorry for myself was very long and depressing. It is hard to pull yourself back together again and start selling with enthusiasm if you are in this place. You will never be as successful again because your whole attitude is jaded.

> *Sometimes the only way to get back on top is to really hit rock bottom. That is when you have to realize what you did wrong and make new decisions.*

No matter how great and successful you were at one point as a sales person, it can happen to anyone.

My friend Tom was a successful stockbroker. His personal net worth was at one point at $22 million because of one successful deal that he was involved in. He spent a lot of money, did even some racecar driving and enjoyed life. He believed that he was set for life and wrote a letter to all his clients telling them that he was going out of the business.

A couple years later the deal crashed and his net worth went from $22 million to zero. He had no more clients and was starting all over again. Unfortunately, he also had a motorcycle accident where he hit his neck and his voice got affected. He had a great and deep voice before and after the accident he sounded a little bit like "mickey mouse" for a while. Now you can imagine how hard this must have been for him. It also took him years to recover from everything and get back on his feet.

> *My advice is to be smart about your money and life in general. Even if you make millions of dollars like I did, don't spend it foolishly. Save your money.*

I blew my money in the most stupid ways and I regret it a lot. Looking back, I should have saved money, bought regular cars and bought more homes. The only thing that is easy about money is to lose it. Even though I was a financial expert with a great income, I still made all the mistakes that you shouldn't make.

How do you recover from a situation like this? You are broke again, live in the past and have no clients and no motivation to make phone calls again.

The solution is: PERSONAL SALES. You need to get back to basics. You need to realize that you have a skill, which is selling and if you use it, you will get results. You need to call up your own clients or simply find new clients and start over. With new results, you will get more motivation. It is the beginning of a positive upward spiral.

I remember when I was in a bad place and was completely broke again. I tried to motivate some former sales people but no one was willing to produce any results. It got so bad that I was under a lot of pressure and my bills were piling up. If I didn't make any money within days, I would lose my house, my cars and the electricity would be shut off.

That day I called up a couple of clients and closed two new deals in one day. I simply did what I could do best, which is selling. I was not concerned with running a business anymore but simply with the process of talking to clients. This was another turning point in my life.

Success through selling

Every successful person is automatically a great sales person and communicator. Once you have understood that principle you will always find a way to be successful – no matter what you do or in which industry you work.

> **Success in sales is a mental game. It is all in your head.**

Success is based on the law of cause and effect. The more cause you set the more results you will get. That is why you must focus your time and energy on the things that will make you money. You must be focused and try to get rid of all the unnecessary tasks and problems that will hinder you from making sales.

If you are down, you must focus on your goals and then go out and take action. Remember: 20% of all of your activities are responsible for 80% of your success.

Another important principle is the reality principle. You cannot live in La-la-land. You must be absolutely realistic with yourself and with your weekly calendar.

Are you really doing everything that you can do to achieve your goals?

The main mental attitude is that there are no excuses.

> *You are responsible for your results.*
> *It is not the market, not the client, not the product or your company.*
> *If you fail, it is no one else's fault but yours.*

Once you have decided to become the best in your field and be absolutely professional in everything that you do, you will rise to new heights.

Self-confidence and fear

> *Once you have overcome your fear of rejection and fear of failure there is nothing that you cannot achieve in sales.*

Because most sales people are afraid of rejection they tend to make less phone calls because it gives them a feeling of insecurity. And because they make less calls, they have less meetings and therefore a poor sales result at the end of the month.

Fear is the main thing that is holding people back. Basically, success in sales is planable. If you are not afraid of rejection or failure and you are not lazy (= have goals that motivate you) then success is inevitable.

The other main factor is self-confidence.

> *The level of your self-confidence will determine how successful you will be.*

There are several ways to increase your level of self-confidence as a sales person:

1. Act as if you were already successful today.
2. Start daily with clear objectives and plans that you write down each day.
3. Take charge of your results. There are no excuses.
4. Focus your energy and time on income producing activities.
5. Develop a sense of urgency.
6. Keep reading and learning every day.
7. Make a commitment to never give up – no matter what happens.

80% of success is based on your attitude and 20% are skills.

Secrets of success as a sales person

1. Learn everything about rhetoric, sales techniques and psychological principles.
2. Use common sense when dealing with people and sales situations.
3. Become a master on the telephone.
4. Create an urgent need for your client so that he has a motivation to change his situation.
5. Always make a product rare and use time pressure.
6. Learn every possible answer to counter objections.
7. Look at your personal goals on a daily basis for 5 minutes.
8. Ask yourself if you have the right mental attitude when it comes to your product and your company. Keep the fire alive inside of you!
9. Continually try to improve yourself and become better.
10. Are you always dressed for success? Do you look the part? If not, change it.

Dedication

This brochure is dedicated to all the sales coaches, managers and sales people that I have encountered over the years. I learned all the basic knowledge about sales from these people:

- David Garcia
- Javier Garcia
- Carsten Maschmeyer
- Jörg Haupt
- Wilhelm Zsifkovits
- Karl Karner
- Brian Tracy
- And many other top sales people and colleagues.

The education about communication and sales that I learned when I was 20 years old was a huge influence on my life and I will always be grateful for this.

I am also grateful for all the sales people that were working for me. I learned a lot from teaching you and I hope that I was also able to positively influence their lives.

And finally, I strongly encourage everyone to read the book "How to win friends and influence people" written by Dale Carnegie. It is a MUST for every sales person.

Printed in the United States
By Bookmasters